Walking with Beasts
A Prehistoric Safari

Written by **Tim Haines**

Picture Designer **Daren Horley**

Walking with Beasts
A Prehistoric Safari

Executive Producer: Tim Haines
Series Producer: Jasper James
Producer: Nigel Paterson

First published by BBC Worldwide Ltd,
Woodlands, 80 Wood Lane
London W12 0TT

ISBN 0-7894-7829-3

Editorial Director: Shirley Patton
Project Editor: Helena Caldon
Text Editor: Caroline Taggart
Cover Art Direction: Pene Parker
Book Art Direction: Linda Blakemore
Book Design: Martin Hendry
Picture Research: Deirdre O'Day
Illustrations: Daren Horley
Maps and diagrams: Matthew Swift and Chris Watson

Set in Fairfield and Franklin Gothic
Printed and bound in Great Britain by Butler & Tanner Ltd, Frome
Colour reproductions by Radstock Reproductions Ltd, Midsomer Norton
Jacket printed by Laurence-Allen Ltd, Weston-super-Mare

DK

Published in the US by
DK Publishing, Inc.
95 Madison Avenue
New York, New York 10016

Snow giant (PAGE 1)
Few ancient mammals are as well-known as the woolly mammoth, indeed its name has entered the language as a byword for size. Odd then that it was in fact smaller than today's African elephant.

Forgotten lives (PREVIOUS PAGES)
Only a million years ago, tropical South America looked very different. Instead of rainforest, there was miles of open plains occupied by strange creatures like the 'hose-nose' macrauchenia and the giant armoured doedicurus which was about the size of a small car.

Contents

1

2

Introduction

Walking with Beasts
A prehistoric safari

Big is beautiful (PREVIOUS PAGES)
The brontotheres of the late Eocene were among the first mammals to get truly enormous, the adults were about the size of elephants.

In the Victorian era, before the vast bone beds of America started churning out dinosaurs, the ancient mammals were the biggest attractions in museums

No escape
Whatever caused the mass extinction 65 million years ago was too much for the dinosaurs, even the mighty Tyrannosaurus. But they were not alone, almost every animal group suffered, mammals just appear to have been better set to recover.

If the history of life on Earth were produced as a Hollywood special it would probably be made into a trilogy. Part one would cover the mysterious Palaeozoic, with its giant insects and armoured fish; the sequel would move on to the majestic Mesozoic, when dinosaurs ruled; and the final instalment would be the spectacular Cenozoic and its age of mammals. Of the three, you would think the climax would be the last one, with its extraordinary beasts and relevance to us humans. Ironically, however, the middle one would probably steal the limelight and people would queue to see its dinosaurs again and again. Even though the more recent Cenozoic has seen the development of all the major groups of mammals and the shaping of our modern world, little about it appears in popular culture. Mention of sabre-toothed cats, mammoths and Neanderthals might raise a nod of recognition, but for some reason the mighty indricothere and terrifying andrewsarchus are not box-office. Yet it wasn't always so. In the Victorian era, before the vast bone beds of America started churning out dinosaurs, the ancient mammals were the biggest attractions in museums.

Walking with Beasts – a prehistoric safari – will bring this forgotten world to life. The creatures you will meet are every bit as exotic and exciting as the dinosaurs – hairy giants that dominated the world for 60 million years before the rise of humans. These were the monstrous ancestors of most of the large animals that share our world today, from waddling early whales to upright ape men.

The Cenozoic era started 65 million years ago with the catastrophic extinction that obliterated the giant dinosaurs and left the birds as the only

legacy of their 170 million-year-old reign. But mammals didn't just take over. It took the world a long time to recover from the KT extinction which saw the end of the dinosaurs and, by the time it was swathed in thick tropical forest about five to ten million years later, many animal groups such as the birds and reptiles were doing well. Mammals, however, were unwittingly laying the foundations for the future. Bats, horses, whales, primates, rodents, hedgehogs, anteaters and others can trace their origins back to these dark, steamy forests. Mammals were nothing if not versatile, and variety was to prove not only the spice of life but the key to success.

They were helped by global changes. The Cenozoic world was a very different place from the one that the dinosaurs knew. Plate tectonics had broken the giant, fused landmasses into several continents, each of which developed distinctive, so-called endemic animals and plants, such as those we see in Australia today. Occasionally these newly formed continents would reconnect and, as the two endemic populations crashed together, natural selection favoured the most adaptable, as happened when North and South America met about three million years ago. Changes in the types of plants were also important. Flowering plants took over in the Cenozoic, replacing the older conifers and ferns. The abundance of flowers affected animal evolution – from honey bees to fruit bats, food gathering probably became a more specialist task than in the bulk bingeing days of the dinosaurs. On top of all this, the climate changed radically, leading to regular shifts in the pattern of vegetation. At first dense forests spread, then they opened out and then they gave way to grasslands. Previously stable equatorial regions started to experience wildly contrasting seasons. And across the millions of years of the Cenozoic age, global temperatures

Mammals were nothing if not versatile, and variety was to prove not only the spice of life but the key to success

Struggle for supremacy
Mammals didn't have it all their own way after the dinosaurs died out. For a time giant carnivorous birds, the direct descendants of the dinosaurs, were the top predators.

11

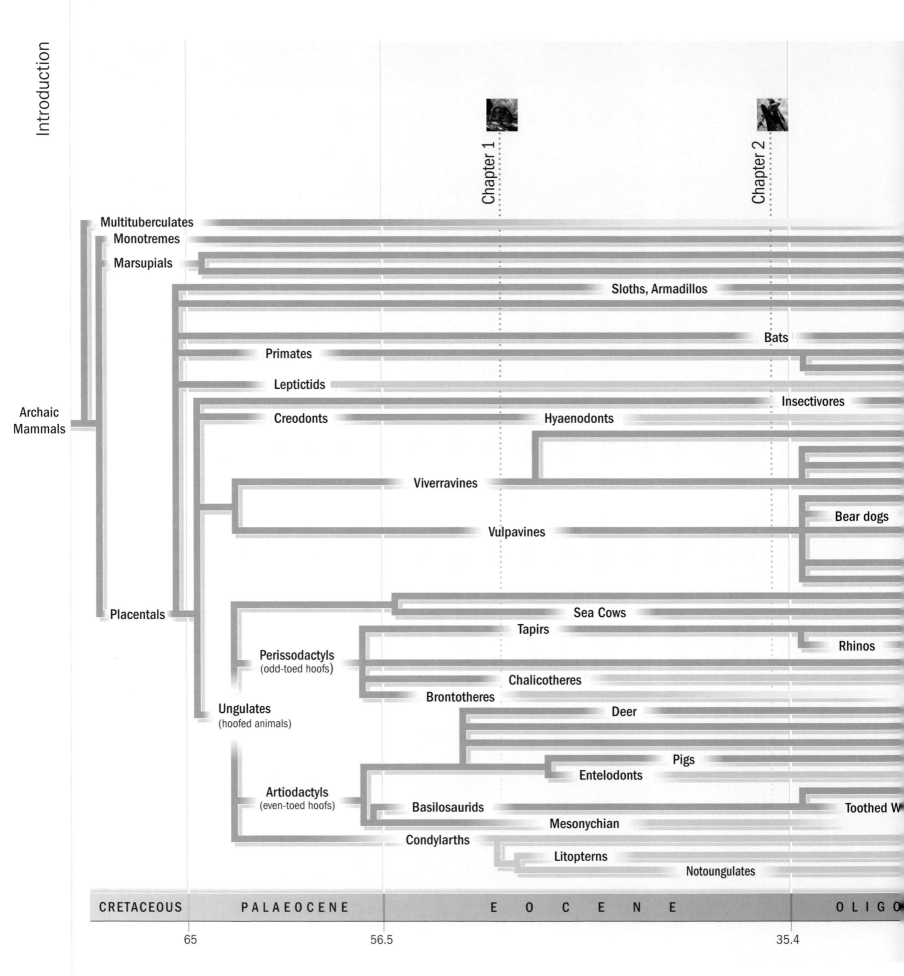

The Ancient Roots of Modern Mammals

During the time of the dinosaurs, many unique groups of small mammals evolved but today there are only three major groups: the monotremes that lay eggs (like the duckbilled platypus), the marsupials that have pouches (like kangaroos) and the placentals who are by far the most dominant and varied group. Although many modern animals, like bats and sloths, have surprisingly ancient ancestors, others, like seals and apes are comparatively recent. The ungulates or 'hoofed' mammals have always been a major group and had their own predatory orders like the mesonychids, but they died out in the Oligocene. Carnivores today are dominated by one group – the Carnivora, which contains everything from cats and dogs to walruses and weasels.

Chapter 3

Chapter 4

Chapter 5

Chapter 6

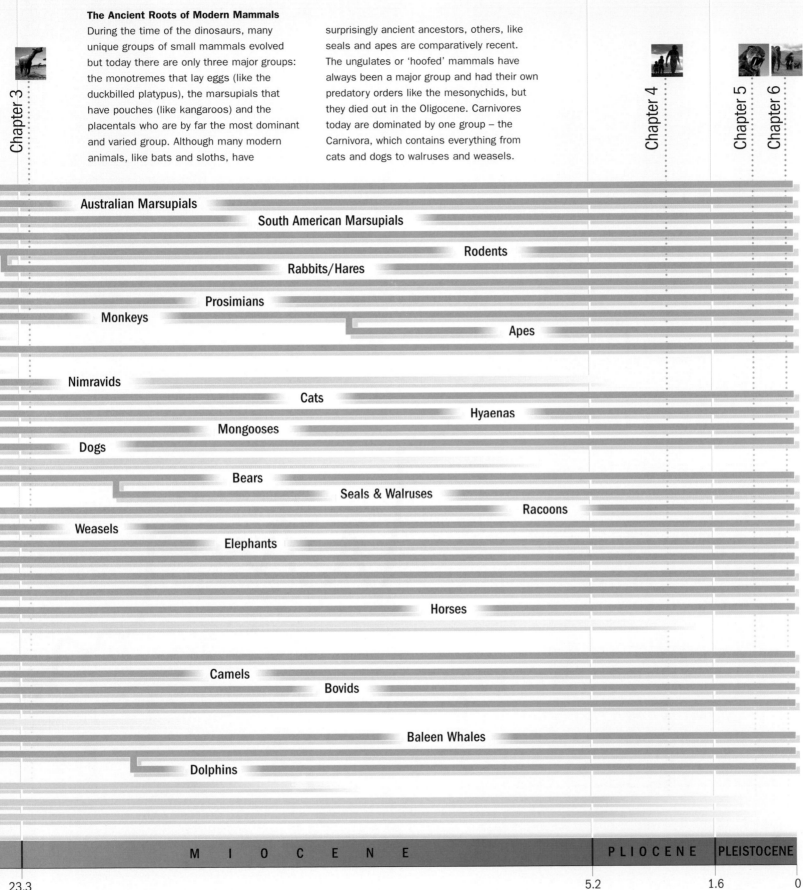

Australian Marsupials

South American Marsupials

Rodents

Rabbits/Hares

Prosimians

Monkeys

Apes

Nimravids

Cats

Hyaenas

Mongooses

Dogs

Bears

Seals & Walruses

Racoons

Weasels

Elephants

Horses

Camels

Bovids

Baleen Whales

Dolphins

M I O C E N E P L I O C E N E PLEISTOCENE

23.3 5.2 1.6 0

Millions of years

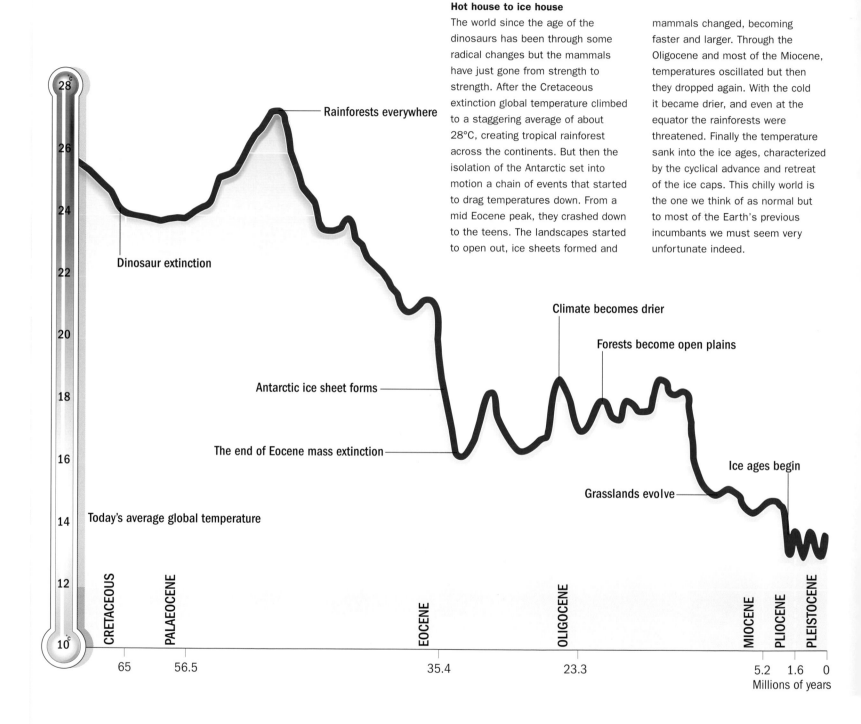

Hot house to ice house

The world since the age of the dinosaurs has been through some radical changes but the mammals have just gone from strength to strength. After the Cretaceous extinction global temperature climbed to a staggering average of about 28°C, creating tropical rainforest across the continents. But then the isolation of the Antarctic set into motion a chain of events that started to drag temperatures down. From a mid Eocene peak, they crashed down to the teens. The landscapes started to open out, ice sheets formed and mammals changed, becoming faster and larger. Through the Oligocene and most of the Miocene, temperatures oscillated but then they dropped again. With the cold it became drier, and even at the equator the rainforests were threatened. Finally the temperature sank into the ice ages, characterized by the cyclical advance and retreat of the ice caps. This chilly world is the one we think of as normal but to most of the Earth's previous incumbents we must seem very unfortunate indeed.

Rainforests everywhere

Dinosaur extinction

Climate becomes drier

Forests become open plains

Antarctic ice sheet forms

The end of Eocene mass extinction

Ice ages begin

Grasslands evolve

Today's average global temperature

28°

26

24

22

20

18

16

14

12

10°

CRETACEOUS

PALAEOCENE

EOCENE

OLIGOCENE

MIOCENE

PLIOCENE

PLEISTOCENE

65 56.5 35.4 23.3 5.2 1.6 0

Millions of years

slid ever downwards until the Earth was flipped into a sequence of punishing ice ages.

Through all these changes mammals seemed to go from strength to strength, and the key to their success was their adaptability. Perhaps surprisingly, nowhere is that clearer than in their teeth. Indeed, it is mostly through the teeth that mammals have left behind in the fossil record that palaeontologists are able to tell different species apart. Mammal teeth were more varied and specialized than those of any other vertebrates, which meant that their owners were able to take advantage of many new food sources, whether their molars were grinding grass or their carnassials

Once they were giants
These gigantic indricotheres were the largest land mammals ever – big enough to rival any dinosaurs. Only 30 million years before, their ancestors were small enough to scamper among the branches.

shearing meat. They even swapped teeth for baleen sieves so that the giant whales could exploit the krill swarms in the polar oceans. Another characteristic that turned out to be a good idea was their fur. This may have seemed unnecessary while global temperatures were tropical, but as temperatures dropped all that hair finally came into its own, enabling creatures such as the musk ox, mammoth and woolly rhino to sit out the grimmest ice-age winter.

So, through versatility and adaptability, creatures that for so many millions of years had been suppressed by the dinosaurs emerged from hiding and grew larger and larger. Eventually mammals came to dominate

Cold-hearted killer
Once the ice ages arrived, mammals' fur came into its own. This cave lion could rely on its coat not only keeping it warm but also by turning white, keeping it camouflaged.

the globe and giants once again roamed the plains. From dinosaur world to furball Earth in a few million years.

Buried in the general evolution of this huge and diverse group of animals is one order in which we as humans take particular interest – the primates. The group from which we evolved. There is no evidence that our distant ancestors ever saw any giant dinosaurs, but ten million years later the trees of the Eocene forests were full of lemur-like prosimians. The trees were the key to primates' early success. In the Cenozoic the three-dimensional world of branches became the proving ground for some of the primates' most distinctive features. Finding food in the canopy and leaping from tree to tree needed good eyesight, grasping hands and the co-ordination to use them. Primates developed these features to perfection and soon the prosimians had been joined by a new group – the monkeys.

One group of primates started to walk upright and finally, a long time after many other types of mammal had done the same, abandoned the trees

As the forests receded, it would appear that primates generally went into decline, but about that time another, heavier group of them evolved. They had no tails and probably spent more time in the lower branches or feeding on the ground. These were the apes. By about four million years ago, in a world now dominated by open grassland, one group of primates started to walk upright and finally, a long time after many other types of mammal had done the same, abandoned the trees. These were the hominids, a group of primates now almost extinct except for one species – humans.

Primates never had an enormous impact on the evolution of mammals until very recently, with our appearance. However, naturally we are interested in them and this presents scientists with a huge challenge, hunting for one tiny group of animals in a fragmented fossil record.

Since the evolution of life is continuous, different continents will exist long after we are gone, harbouring different animals and labouring under completely different climatic conditions. But it is worth considering how our present time might be characterized by future palaeontologists. For a start, despite fears of global warming, we have come into being during the coldest time for hundreds of millions of years. On top of this, all that water locked up in the ice caps and the present course of ocean currents mean it is also very dry. In botanical terms it is no coincidence that agriculture mostly grows grass crops and rears grazing animals. Helped by the dry cold conditions grasses are probably one of the most successful plants in Earth's history and, as far as the future scientist is concerned, could be viewed as the dominant organisms of our age.

A new race
An upright stance is what first separated man from other apes and one theory suggests this evolved as the forests they lived in became more and more open, forcing them to spend more time on the ground.

Our Distant Primate Cousins

Despite being very recently evolved creatures, our family history goes right back. The very earliest primates appeared with many other new types of mammal in the early Eocene forests. They were probably mostly nocturnal and looked a bit like modern lemurs. Yet, despite their relatively large brains, forward facing eyes and grasping hands, they didn't immediately take over the world. Primate evolution continued quietly to progress, we were one of many groups that thrived through the Eocene. By the Oligocene, monkeys had appeared and there is strong evidence many were sociable, daylight creatures. During the Oligocene, apes also evolved and these three types – apes, monkeys and prosimians – remained the only major groups until hominids arrived 4.5 million years ago. Since then all the hominids have died out except for one: *Homo sapiens* – ourselves.

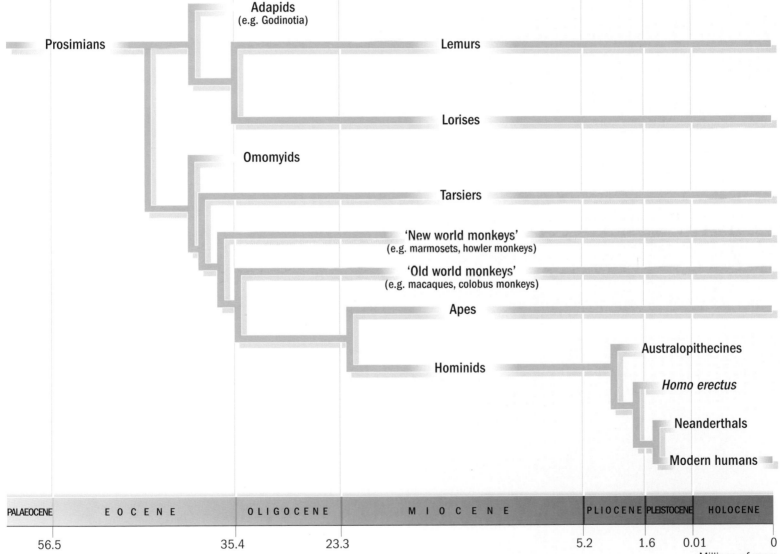

PALAEOCENE	E O C E N E	OLIGOCENE	M I O C E N E	PLIOCENE	PLEISTOCENE	HOLOCENE

56.5   35.4   23.3   5.2   1.6   0.01   0

Millions of years

Labels within figure: Prosimians; Adapids (e.g. Godinotia); Lemurs; Lorises; Omomyids; Tarsiers; 'New world monkeys' (e.g. marmosets, howler monkeys); 'Old world monkeys' (e.g. macaques, colobus monkeys); Apes; Hominids; Australopithecines; *Homo erectus*; Neanderthals; Modern humans

Cat food
Early hominids showed no signs that their descendants would become the planet's top predator. Australopithecines were just as likely to end up as the dinner of a sabre-tooth cat like dinofelis as the nearest antelope.

We, of course, have influenced evolution very recently, mostly through creating environments that favour certain organisms, such as grasses, rats and pigeons, but that work against others, such as pandas, tigers and rhinos. But there is one other distinctive feature of our time. Although through most of the Cenozoic land mammals have evolved numerous large species, we live in a world of comparative midgets. With the exception of the elephants and rhinos of Africa and India, most continents have lost their giant creatures in the last few thousand years. Woolly rhinos, mammoths, giant sloths, giant marsupials and even the giant moa birds of New Zealand are all recent extinctions. Could this be our fault?

That theory may fit with current feelings of environmental guilt, but actually many of the extinctions occurred while we were still wearing furs and presenting an easy target for a hungry cat. Although we may have been a major factor more recently, it is hard to see how a few thousand early Cro-magnons could have

Through most of the Cenozoic mammals have evolved numerous large species, we live in a world of comparative midgets

managed to wipe out hundreds of thousands of mammoths, especially since there is hardly any evidence that our ancestors actively hunted these huge woolly creatures in the first place. There must have been other forces at work. The rapid switching between ice ages and warmer interglacial periods is a likely culprit; since larger animals find it more difficult to cope with swiftly changing environments, this could have selectively culled them. But whatever the reason future scientists decide explains why our giants are missing, it is sadly our loss that we have so few to wonder at. Maybe our modern fascination with monstrous creatures from the past is fed by their absence today. If so, I hope this book goes some way to giving you an idea of what it must have been like to live amongst giants.

1 New Dawn

Our world 49 million years ago

It is 15 million years since the mass extinction that saw the end of the dinosaurs. All evidence of the environmental havoc left by this event has been erased from the Earth's surface. This is the Eocene or 'dawn of new times'. The Earth is now a forest planet – a lush green paradise covered in tropical and sub-tropical jungle. Sea levels and global temperatures are high – you could swim in the Arctic Sea and magnolias thrive in Alaska. The spread of flowering plants that started in the dinosaurs' era has continued and the forests are now full of fruit, flowers and scents. Among the larger vertebrates the influence of the dinosaurs lives on. The mammals have not been quick to occupy the new niches and no large predators have evolved to replace the giant reptiles. Instead, crocodiles hunt along the waterways and huge predatory birds comb the forests for prey. But mammals are better prepared for the future; they remain small and have begun to diversify. In the forests, there are the first primates, rodents, hoofed plant-eaters, carnivores and bats.

5 a.m. The quiet time The Eocene jungle is very still just before sunrise. Around a dark lake the forest stacks up in dense green layers washed with an opaque pre-dawn light. A few bats flap silently between the upper branches, making their way back to their roosts. The hum from insects seems muted and the occasional haunting screech from a primate in the canopy only emphasizes the silence. Suddenly ripples spread across the surface of the lake and waves appear from nowhere. There is a low rumble, which sends birds squawking from the trees and mammals scuttling through the undergrowth. A series of huge bubbles erupts from the lake, producing a small, sickly white cloud of gas. Beneath it the water stains red. Then it is over – a short earthquake that leaves the denizens of the forest jumpy but unharmed.

A series of huge bubbles erupts from the lake, producing a small, sickly white cloud of gas

Life is sweet (PREVIOUS PAGES) In the newly-evolved tropical forests which clothe the Earth, small mammals, such as these propalaeotherium, distant ancestors of the horse, grow fat on fruits and flowers.

Tremors are common here because the lake sits on a large island in the middle of the western Tethys Sea. To the north lies the giant Eurasian continent and to the south, Africa is slowly drifting northwards, squeezing the Tethys in between and causing volcanic activity across the area. The lake itself is the reason for the bubbles and gas. This is its dark secret. It is about 2 kilometres (1.2 miles) across and more than 200 metres (650 feet) deep in places. At the very bottom is a dense layer of cold water trapped under a thick layer of warmer water. The cold water is stagnant and full of dissolved carbon dioxide. Every so often gas levels build up to such an extent that, when a tremor mixes the two layers, it can trigger the release of clouds of suffocating carbon dioxide which drift towards the shore. This all makes the lake a very dangerous neighbour.

On this morning the cloud released is small, but its effects are deadly. A bat swoops low over the water, plucking a caddis fly out of the air, but as it turns it heads into the cloud of gas. After a few metres its delicate wings crumple and it drops with a small plop into the water. As the cloud reaches the reed and lily beds on the eastern shore it is already beginning to disperse. A palaeotis bird sitting on her nest opens her beak in a silent scream as she is suddenly robbed of oxygen. She shakes her head vigorously and staggers to her feet. Before the cloud can finish the job, it is carried on into the fern and palm stands beyond on the morning breeze. The palaeotis puffs her dark brown plumage and settles back on her nest a little confused.

The cloud finally disperses as the ground rises. Here, where the understorey thins beneath huge laurel trees, the leaf litter has been scraped into a huge mound and topped with sticks and branches. Sitting on top of this, making a strange throaty whistle as she sleeps, is a gastornis. She is the largest bird on Earth, a carnivorous giant about

Gastornis
A huge, heavily built, flightless bird, one of the largest animals around at the time and a fierce ambush predator.
EVIDENCE: Only the imprint of a single thigh bone of *Gastornis* has been found in the Messel shales near Frankfurt (see pages 56–7), but they are common at the nearby site of Geiseltal and in the USA.
SIZE: 1.75 metres (5 feet 9 inches) tall.
DIET: Meat, either hunted or scavenged.
TIME: 56–41 million years ago.

Heart of darkness
Today the frozen poles have
confined rainforests to the
tropics, but in the Eocene
they covered the world.

Small is beautiful

By the middle Eocene, life was a jungle.
During the 15 million years since the
dinosaur extinction, the global climate had
been getting steadily warmer and more
humid, returning weather conditions on
Earth to something like the balmy days of
the middle Mesozoic. Flowering plants and
tropical rainforest dominated the planet.

This seems to have limited the size of
many animals. Nearly all the land mammals
were small, their size perhaps restricted by

a lack of space in the dense forests. Only
the birds managed to produce a gigantic
flightless predator in the form of the
widespread and abundant *Gastornis*.

The continents of the Earth had formed
themselves in two broad regions. In the
north there was a single landmass
comprising what is now North America,
Europe, Asia and Africa. To the south lay
South America, Antarctica and Australia,
joined together but separated from the
northern continents. As Antarctica was still
free of ice, the animals were able to roam
widely in the south. There were also several
island subcontinents, the most notable of
which were India, which had yet to join with
Asia, and Madagascar. Both were moving
eastwards away from the African mainland.

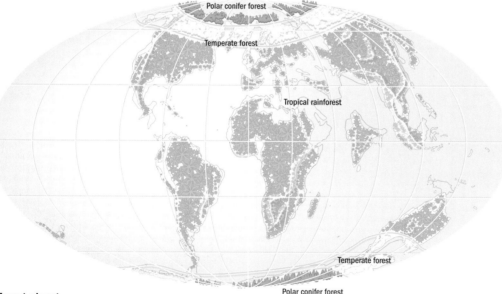

Forest planet
There probably has never been a time when the
Earth looked verdant. Except for the far north and
south, every continent was covered in tropical
vegetation. The continued presence of the Tethys
Sea, the lack of ice caps and the high sea levels

ensured rainfall was high on all continents. A huge
range of newly-evolved, broad-leaved, flowering
trees filled these forests, providing much food for
the various mammals but also, because of their
density, keeping the animals they supported small.

Early success
Although they are highly specialized, it seems bats
were one of the first distinctive modern mammal
groups to evolve.

In North America and Europe the rainforests dominated the landscape. A wide variety of animal life had adapted itself to the abundant food supplies in the jungles. On the forest floor were the first representatives of the recently evolved hoofed animals such as the small horse *Propalaeotherium,* the scaly pangolins and the enigmatic group of insectivorous animals known as the leptictids. They were stalked by hunters such as the creodonts, small carnivorous mammals, crocodiles and *Gastornis.* Higher up in the trees there were rodents scurrying along the branches and early primates, an animal group whose dextrous ability to live in trees is ideally suited to the forest world. For the first time, some mammals had forsaken the ground

Weird and weirder
Most mammals have changed radically since the Eocene, but a few, like the pangolin, seem to have remained the same for 50 million years.

altogether and chosen to hunt insects on the wing. These were the bats, whose sudden appearance in the fossil record leaves their origins shrouded in mystery.

While the northern hemisphere was dominated by the evolutionary success of the placental mammals, who carried their offspring to term inside their bodies, in the

At the North Pole there were no ice caps. Instead there was an ocean with two distinct seasons

south these creatures were rare. In their place were a unique group of marsupial mammals, who used a pouch to carry their young for the latter part of the pregnancy and whose isolation from the northern placentals ensured their success for tens of millions of years to come. Although the mammals' success was noteworthy, they were not alone in seizing their chances after the death of the dinosaurs. The birds too started to spread their evolutionary wings, creating the forerunners to many modern forms including pigeons, owls and cuckoos.

In a world of high sea levels, marine creatures were also doing well. The warm climate meant that complex coral reef

ecosystems could be found far outside the tropics. On them life continued much as it had on reefs everywhere for millions of years. Off shore the sharks were the top predators, a situation that would shortly change when the first fully aquatic whales evolved. At the North Pole there were no ice caps. Instead there was an ocean with two distinct seasons – a sunlit summer full of rich plankton and fish, and a winter of total darkness when the plankton died back and the fish hibernated.

The middle Eocene was a key period in recent evolutionary history. Never again would global temperatures be this high. Mammals were diversifying, laying the foundations for some of the modern world's most successful animal lineages.

The test of time
Crocodiles survived the death of the dinosaurs and briefly broke out of their semi-aquatic niche, to evolve into running terrestrial forms.

2 metres (6.5 feet) tall, with a stout, muscular body. She cannot fly, but instead ambushes her prey amongst the dense undergrowth. In the dim light the shape of her huge body is hard to make out under her speckled black feathers, but there is no mistaking her livid red features and pale beak. The beak, in particular, is an awesome sight – a thick hatchet-shaped weapon that can snap the backbone of a small horse in one bite. She is queen of the jungle.

The gastornis was undisturbed by the tremor and oblivious to the gas cloud. She is a day-time hunter and slumbers through the night, stirring only at dawn. All around her in the forest other diurnal creatures sleep on, unaware of the close brush some have had with death.

6 a.m. A dawn start Sunrise and, because of rain in the night, the forest begins to steam. High in the canopy a thick mist hangs between the trees, tinged orange by the dawn light. Lower down, the branches and leaves splinter the light into rays that pierce through the dark forest floor. A little distance from the lake a huge strangler fig stands lashed to the ground by its web of branches. Deep inside, the laurel tree it originally grew on has long since been killed. This makes a perfect shelter for a mother leptictidium and her two babies. Her nest, raised well off the ground, is dry and the entrance protected by an impossible maze of fig roots. Inside, the family are preparing for their morning hunt. Leptictidium are creatures of habit and the day always starts with a frantic washing session. The mother's long pink nose twitches as she works methodically over her soft brown fur. As she shifts to an inspection of her long hopping feet her youngsters play with her naked tail. After one of them nips it, she stops grooming and scrambles out into the moist morning air. The youngsters follow obediently. Leptictidium are common in this forest and several different species can be seen bounding through the undergrowth after insects and lizards. This mother

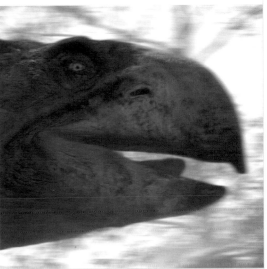

The gastornis's instrument of death is its beak. While most birds use theirs to get at seeds and berries, this fearsome hatchet is designed to crush backbones.

Top predator
Stepping into the niche vacated by the dinosaurs, the giant carnivorous bird gastornis is heavily built and monstrously powerful, compared to its delicate flying cousins.

29

In the dinosaurs' footsteps

During the nineteenth century odd bits and pieces of fossil bone were found from a species of gigantic flightless bird that lived during the Palaeocene and Eocene epochs. Scientists called this bird *Gastornis*, their fully reconstructed skeletons standing over 2.2 metres (7 feet) tall with powerful and sharp beaks. The body could have weighed as much as half a tonne. This was a truly massive beast built to rule the jungles of the early Cenozoic.

The shape of its beak and heavy muscular body suggested that *Gastornis* was carnivorous and in its day it would have been by far the largest meat-eating animal on land. Its powerful build would have prevented it from running at speed and so it probably hid in wait before rushing out and grabbing passing prey with its powerful beak. It is almost certain that some of the ancestors of today's mammals were on the menu for *Gastornis*.

Gastornis's diet has attracted a good deal of scientific controversy in recent years, since researchers at the American Museum of Natural History suggested that *Gastornis* was not a fierce hunter but ate fruit and seeds instead. Their argument was based mostly on the shape of the beak, which they thought could be better used for crushing husks and nuts than for tearing meat. However, two other palaeontologists, Larry Witmer and Kenneth Rose, carried out a detailed analysis of *Gastornis*'s beak and concluded that it was more suited for dealing with meat and that the massively powerful jaw muscles could only have been used to crush bone. Currently, most people favour the view that *Gastornis* was a predator.

It is almost certain that some of the ancestors of today's mammals were on the menu for *Gastornis*

Although *Gastornis* reigned supreme over much of the Earth for nearly 20 million years, about 40 million years ago it started to disappear. Other birds evolved giant species, but with the evolution of large mammalian carnivores they would never again be the top predators. You could say that this was when dinosaurs at last surrendered the predatory niche they had occupied for almost 200 million years.

Big bird
Gastornis was not built for speed; its massive skeleton suggests it was an ambush predator.

belongs to the largest species, measuring almost a metre from her nose to the tip of her tail. She pauses for a moment to sniff for danger and then bounces off through the fig roots. On a branch an owl puffs up its long ribbon-like plumage and watches them go.

All leptictidium have a hunting trail that they follow through the undergrowth. Every morning and evening they work their way round the trail – catching food and clearing any obstacle that falls across their path. Should a predator ambush them, these trails become their escape routes. Today they will be used well. The three little mammals move swiftly through the steamy forest floor bouncing on their long back legs. The trail takes them down towards the lake and on to a small silt beach.

Leptictidium
These strange, hopping animals were part of a group that survived the great extinction at the end of the Cretaceous, but became extinct as the great tropical forests opened up at the beginning of the Oligocene. Three species are well preserved in the Messel shales, with outlines of fur and stomach contents.
EVIDENCE: The leptictids were a widespread group and were around for a long time. *Leptictidium* itself was a specialized hopper with the best preserved specimens found in the Messel shales.
SIZE: Up to 90 centimetres (3 feet) long.
DIET: Small lizards, small mammals and invertebrates.
TIME: 50–40 million years ago.

Sign of the times
Leptictidium are typical of the mammals that infest the forest – small, fast furballs that invest a lot in rearing their young.

The mother stops for a moment, then snaps at a large stag beetle on a log. She holds the wriggling insect firmly in her hands, while her sharp teeth make short work of it. The youngsters gather round to taste the food from her lips. It is just two weeks since they were born and they are already being weaned. They must learn quickly how to hunt for themselves.

Their progress slows as they near the lake, with the mother finding more insects on which to feed. The trail also takes them along the top of the beach and, in this more exposed environment, the mother stops frequently to check for danger. There is a quiet in the air and her nose and whiskers quiver nervously.

It turns out her caution is justified. A brief flash of red in a nearby tea bush is followed by the snap of a branch and the female gastornis bursts from her hiding place. In three strides she is on her prey, snatching at them with resounding cracks of her huge beak. But the leptictidium started moving the moment the mother saw the flash of red and, bounding at full pelt, they just escape the lethal beak. With astonishing speed they head back up their trail through the fig roots and into the safety of their nest. The gastornis is left standing and, after a couple more strides, she loses interest in the hunt. She is too big to be a pursuit predator here; she relies more on ambush amid the dense forest.

The gastornis turns and struts down to the lake shore. With a low mist swirling round her clawed feet, her black speckled plumage and her menacing red-stained face, her distinguished ancestry is clear. She is a return to the age of carnivorous therapod dinosaurs, giant killers that once stalked the land on two legs. But in this new age she is a creature out of time. There are many other predators around, such as walking crocodiles and small but powerful creodont mammals. The gastornis is the biggest of all of them, but in contrast to the time of the dinosaurs there are no giant herbivores for her to feast on. She has to work hard for her living.

Forest ambush
Leptictidium's powerful back legs help it not only to leap after insects, but also to escape attack by predators such as gastornis.

9 a.m. End of the first shift By mid morning the mist is long gone and the combination of high sun and dense greenery makes the air stiflingly humid. The forest here is typical of the tropical jungle that swathes most of this warm planet. The flowering plants that only started their evolution towards the end of the time of the dinosaurs are now dominant. Although a few ferns and cypresses hold on, the canopy is full of laurel, walnut, beech palm and dogwood. Climbers such as grapevines, honeysuckles and moonseeds wrap round these trees, while below magnolias, mulberries, tea and citrus bushes fight for light.

The variety on display is bewildering, but the things that would really confuse a time-travelling dinosaur are the colours and the smells. The jungle is full of flowers and fruits, and in the morning heat their scent is overpowering. The green and brown dinosaur world of ferns and conifer needles has gone for ever. This seismic change in the flora is reflected in the type of animals that thrive here. The canopy is abuzz with wasps and bees. Among the branches and on the ground small mammals and birds grow fat on a diet of large fruit

This is a new Eden, a colourful scented world full of small animals – completely different from the age of the dinosaurs

and soft flowers – gone is most of the rough, resin-filled fare on which dinosaur plant eaters had to survive. This is a new Eden, a colourful scented world full of small animals – completely different from the age of the dinosaurs.

Under the canopy the darkness is broken by patches of magnesium-white light, where the sun breaks through to the forest floor. A timid propalaeotherium horse tugs at a moonseed illuminated by one such ray of light. He is keen to draw it into the shadows where his dark dappled back will provide the security of camouflage.

A scuffle at the edge of the clearing sends the propalaeotherium scampering off. The leptictidium mother arrives and stops to wrestle with a lizard she has caught. The two youngsters catch up and join in. Suddenly the lizard's brightly coloured tail pops off and starts to thrash about among the leaves. The youngsters leap back, pause and then pursue the tail with a series of hunting moves they have seen their mother perform. She meanwhile, holds tightly on to the lizard's body and, after a firm bite to the back of the neck, it goes limp. She then heads off again for the nest. The youngsters follow, abandoning the tail to flick around by itself.

Propalaeotherium

These little forest animals are among the earliest horses known. They belong to the perissodactyls – a group which also includes tapirs and rhinoceros. Living in thick forest, they had four little hooves on their front feet and three on the back, and walked on pads, like dogs or cats.

EVIDENCE: More than 35 beautifully preserved specimens of the two species are known from the Messel shales, and they have also been found at the nearby site of Geiseltal.

SIZE: Two species, one 30–35 centimetres (12–14 inches) at the shoulder, the other 55–60 centimetres (22–24 inches).

DIET: Browsed on leaves and also ate fallen fruits.

TIME:: 49–43 million years ago.

Bird food

Propalaeotherium are skittish, nervous herbivores whose only defence against large predators is to run away.

Ambulocetus
Although *Ambulocetus* looked rather like a huge otter, it was in fact one of the earliest whales. Less agile in the water than an otter, it seems to have been adapted for ambushing large prey, which it then drowned.
EVIDENCE: One fairly complete specimen and several partial skeletons have been found in Pakistan.
SIZE: 3 metres (10 feet) long.
DIET: Carnivorous.
TIME: 49–50 million years ago.

It is the end of the leptictidiums' morning hunt and the family disappear under the strangler fig for their midday sleep. Inside the nest the mother finishes eating the lizard – although the youngsters will learn to hunt from her, she will never kill prey for them. They continue to try to suckle, but she is rapidly losing patience. Their time within her nest is running out – they will soon have to learn to be independent. For now, however, they all curl up and go to sleep.

Down by the lake, swifts dart across the surface, striking at the columns of mating insects. A python slips through the water lilies, heading for shore to digest a baby crocodile it has just caught. Nearby a much larger wake also heads for the shore. Just before it reaches the bank there is a splash and the top of a long brown head pops out of the water. At a glance it could be mistaken for a large crocodile, since there are plenty of those in the lake. But a closer look reveals that it is covered in a layer of fur and that there are whiskers bristling round its dark nose. Its eyes scan the bank and then, as it draws itself out on to the silt, it becomes clear that this extraordinary beast is nothing like a crocodile. Thick short hair covers its entire body and large webbed feet make it move awkwardly on land. This is a male ambulocetus, part of a bizarre group of mammals that have evolved to take advantage of a similar niche to crocodiles, hunting animals along the water's edge. Ambulocetus evolved on the Eurasian coast to the east of this forest and it is very rare to see one on the European islands. However, the jungle round the lake is full of bite-sized prey, so it should not be short of food.

This male is about 3 metres (10 feet) long, not quite fully grown. He slides into position, half in and half out of the water, in a patch of sedge that disguises his body. Then he settles down and waits. The ambulocetus's hunting method requires a lot of patience. They have developed a special jaw and ear apparatus that is very sensitive to

A close shave

When the evolution of the horse was first investigated in the 1870s the story seemed quite straightforward – small, many-toed 'dawn' horse grows up into familiar single-hoofed *Equus*. But now that scientists know more, it appears that *Equus* was just a lucky survivor from a much larger group of animals and not typical of them at all.

The earliest known horse was a small animal feeding on soft fruit and leaves in the great forests which covered much of the Eocene world. It had four toes on its front feet and three on the back, and walked softly on dog-like pads.

As the forests began to shrink, these horses came under pressure. Those with teeth better suited to tougher vegetation began to diversify. The original early forest-dwellers, such as *Propalaeotherium*, became extinct and they were replaced by descendants of the tougher-teethed horses, such as *Miohippus*. On the plains, another group of descendants adapted to eat the grasses which were beginning to dominate the open spaces.

Eventually, about 15 million years ago, all the forest-living horses became extinct, but the plains-living horses were doing very well. There was a huge diversity of shapes and forms. Most had three toes on both the front and back feet, but some plains-living runners started to lose the side toes and put all their weight on the central toe. Both these types did very well for a time, but gradually competition from herbivores

A horse tale
After millions of years of success, the horse almost became extinct, but thanks to us humans they are now as widespread as ever.

such as antelope and deer reduced their success and by 4 million years ago only one kind was left – *Equus*. Any environmental campaign at that time might well have bemoaned the passing of such an illustrious and varied group of animals.

Equus itself had a close shave: it only just made it into modern times by hopping continents. For some reason (perhaps climate change, or overhunting by newly arrived humans) all the horses of the Americas, where most had evolved, died out. However, *Equus* species had managed to cross into Asia during one of the first Ice Ages, 2.6 million years ago, where they remained. Eventually humans and horses struck up a relationship, ensuring their survival. Humans started to breed and protect horses and once again they spread around the world.

A bright future
Some superb fossils of primitive horses from the Eocene have allowed scientists to trace precisely the evolution of the single hoof.

Silent running
A clumsy waddling creature on land, ambulocetus is graceful under water, undulating its body up and down like an otter.

The teeth of ambulocetus are ideal for grabbing and dragging victims off riverbanks into the water. They also betray its ancestors as the terrestrial predators called mesonychians.

vibration. By resting their head on the ground they can sense the approach of prey and time their attack perfectly. Unfortunately, this does mean they have to wait for their victims to come to them.

In the oppressive heat of mid-morning the ambulocetus starts his unique vigil. A huge flying ant lands on his forehead and explores the drying fur round his neck, but he does not move. After about half an hour a propalaeotherium appears from the undergrowth. She stands motionless in the shadows, her ears twitching. Then she nervously picks her way down to the lake to drink. Every few sips she looks around, alert to the slightest moves that would betray a predator. She is drinking just 2 metres (6.5 feet) from the stationary ambulocetus, but that is still too far for his purposes. Only when a large splash among the lilies sends the little horse jumping back does the predator make his move. With a flurry of dust and leaves, a huge fang-filled mouth slashes sideways. But the horse was never near enough and, leaping high into the air, she disappears off into the jungle.

The ambulocetus decides to abandon his hunting, as the daytime temperatures are getting too high. He turns and slips into the water. After pushing off from the shore, a few sweeps of his webbed feet bring him to the deep, dark water that occupies most of the lake. Then his body and short tail fall into a series of slow, up-and-down undulations that propel him through the water without the use of his limbs. This movement is very distinctive of these new semi-aquatic mammals and will one day be the trademark of their descendants, the whales. Below the ambulocetus, a crocodile moves past, its tail beating from side to side. The two do not bother each other.

Only when a large splash among the lilies sends the little horse jumping back does the predator make his move

Monster mouth (OVERLEAF)
A tiny horse is surprised by what erupts out of his drinking water. Fortunately, his lightning-fast reactions save him.

39

12 noon. The swarming In the direct sunlight the temperature continues to climb into the blistering 40s, but under the shade of the canopy it peaks in the lower 30s. In their strangler-fig nest the leptictidium no longer lie bundled together: instead they are stretched out, breathing fast to keep cool. Beneath the laurel with its massive buttressed roots, the gastornis has returned to her nest. In the centre lies a single large blue-green egg which she has been incubating for weeks. Today for the first time it is making a noise. With her fearsome beak she gently turns it, revealing a small hole worked by the chick as it starts the monumental task of breaking out of its shell prison. The pointed end of a small yellow beak appears in the hole and then a round purple tongue accompanied by a sharp rasping call. The mother gastornis will not assist in this hatching, which could take the chick several hours; instead she checks round her nest for intruders and heads back into the forest to find fresh meat for her new arrival.

About 50 metres (160 feet) away from the nest and deeper into the forest, a propalaeotherium is enjoying a harvest of overripe grapes. Although only 60 centimetres (2 feet) long, he stands on his hind legs and reaches up over a metre to gorge himself on the mouldy clusters hanging off the vine. His little hoofed paws are incapable of grasping anything, but he can easily pluck the fruit with his muzzle. Suddenly he drops and freezes, his ears rigid. Despite the blistering temperatures and the clear blue sky above, he can hear a sound like gentle rain. Slowly it gets louder and the horse bolts. Soon the forest floor has spiders and large insects, such as cockroaches and grasshoppers, scrambling after the larger animals.

Eventually the reason for the panic and the sound of rain becomes apparent. From around the laurel bough that supports the vine comes a column of giant ants. Soon the area where the propalaeotherium was standing is swarming with thousands of these ruthless hunters, tumbling over one another in a dark red tide as they search for fresh meat.

Soft spot

Just like the dinosaurs millions of years ago, for a gastornis the most vulnerable stage of its life is when it is incubating in or hatching in a nest on the ground.

Pretty boy

Once out of the egg, hatchling gastornis grow fast on a diet of meat. The sooner they can escape the confines of the nest, the better.

The killer swarm

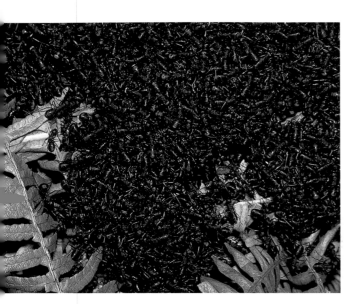

Colonial life
Ants are among the most socially sophisticated of all insects and by attacking as a colony, they can bring down prey thousands of times their weight.

Although it might sound like something out of a horror movie, one of the creatures for which the Messel shales (see pages 56–7) are famous is the giant ant. Insect fossils are rare, since insects tend to be small and have no bones to fossilize. But in the still, stagnant mud of the Messel they were beautifully preserved – beetles still gleamed with their original iridescent colours, and even delicate wings were traced on the clay.

Probably the most exciting insect finds in the Messel shales and the nearby Eckfeld Maar were ants. Only the winged sexual forms (familiar as swarms on late summer evenings in Europe) have so far been found, possibly because the smaller, non-winged workers could walk on water

have a well-developed mechanism for closing off the crop, implying that they could not store liquid food in it, as most modern ants can. Instead, it appeared that they fed on solid food – either as leaf cutters (which use leaves to farm fungus colonies for food) or as carnivores, like the modern driver or army ants. Comparisons with their closest living relatives, such as the European Red Wood Ant, *Formica rufa*, make it seem more likely that they were carnivorous. Given the ferocity of the attack of modern carnivorous ants, which are only around 1 centimetre (less than ½ inch long), a swarm of these giants moving through the forest must have been a nightmare for any animal unable to get out of the way.

A swarm of these giants moving through the Eocene forest must have been a nightmare for any animal that couldn't get out of the way

and were therefore less likely to drown and be preserved. Some winged females were enormous, with a wingspan of up to 13 centimetres (5 inches) and weighing several times more than the smallest modern hummingbirds.

By examining the ants' guts in close detail, scientists found that the ants did not

Giant among insects
This male has a wingspan of about 13 centimetres. He belongs to a colony of hundreds and thousands. Maybe *Gastornis* was not the top predator after all.

They vary in size, with the largest being over 3 centimetres (1 inch) but *en masse* they can bring down surprisingly large prey. The sound of rain comes from the thousands of ants that have scaled the trees and bushes in the search for victims and, if not successful, simply dropped back down to rejoin their merciless colleagues. The swarm is the end of a long column that stretches 50 metres (160 feet) back to the buttress roots of an old walnut tree. Here a mass of ants form a temporary nest that protects their queen. Along the column countless hunters are bringing trophies back to the nest – grubs, beetles, grasshopper legs, even a bat's wing.

All through the midday heat this devastating group predator works its way across the forest floor, methodically dismembering anything that cannot move out of the way. Soon the ants reach the gigantic strangler fig. The main column moves by, but individual outriders stay to explore the roots. Inside the strangler the leptictidium mother sleeps with her young, unaware of the danger outside. More and more ants forage amongst the roots. Despite the leptictidium's size, if hundreds of giant ants fill the entrance to her nest she and her young will be lucky to survive.

After about ten minutes the number of ants around the fig decreases. In the column small bits of bloodied black feathers are being carried back to the nest. The swarm has discovered the gastornis nest 30 metres (100 feet) away. Ever since the ants arrived in the area this has been a danger. If they had come across the nest while the egg was still intact, the chick would probably have been unharmed, but now it is hatching and the small window it has opened in the shell lets in its killers. Even if the mother had been present there would have been little she could do. By now the swarm has covered the huge nest and there is frantic activity around the egg itself. For the chick, it is a slow and nightmarish death.

The leptictidium sleep on, but as long as the giant ant nest remains they are at risk. Tomorrow there will be no chick to distract the swarm.

Giant ants

Insects are a very ancient group, going back well before the dinosaurs, and during the Cretaceous period the first social ants started to make colonies. The Eocene giants, *Formicium gigantcum*, are the largest ants ever found, and their colonies must have had a dramatic impact on the life of the forest. Their carnivorous habits may have made them the equivalent of modern driver or army ants, which are important predators in today's tropical forests.

EVIDENCE: Fossils of *Formicium giganteum* have been found in the Messel shales and a very similar species in the nearby Eckfeld Maar.

SIZE: Workcrs 1–3 centimetres (⅓–over 1 inch) long, but queens 5.5 centimetres (2 inches) long with a wingspan of 13 centimetres (5 inches), bigger than some birds.

DIET: Carnivorous, eating any animal that could not get out of their way.

TIME: 49–44 million years ago.

4 p.m. After the heat By late afternoon the worst of the heat is over and the general level of activity among the forest animals increases. The leptictidium wake and, after a short grooming and licking session, set out again to hunt. The ant column is still moving bits of gastornis chick past the fig and one of the youngsters receives the unwanted attention of a couple of ants. He bounces up and down, twisting in the air in his efforts to shake them off. With some difficulty he follows his mother down a track away from the swarm. But the more persistent ants cling on and later will be eaten by the mother.

On the way they pass a pair of propalaeotherium. Unusually, the horses seem unconcerned by the sudden appearance of the leptictidium. In fact, their responses seem altogether slower and their balance is poor. For the last hour or so they have been feeding on rotting grapes they have found on the forest floor. Now that they have stomachs full of fermenting fruit, alcohol has entered their bloodstream.

Like a black nightmare the gastornis is swiftly upon them. Scrambling and falling, one horse manages to escape into the undergrowth, but the nearer one has no chance

This is not a good time to get drunk. Other creatures, as well as the leptictidium, are out hunting in the late afternoon. The gastornis has been moving slowly towards the horses through the dark forest shadows. Now only 10 metres (30 feet) away, she is ready to strike.

The propalaeotherium sense something and try to run, but their reactions are slow and confused. Like a black nightmare the gastornis is swiftly upon them. Scrambling and falling, one horse manages to escape into the undergrowth, but the nearer one has no chance. The huge beak closes right across his back and lifts him clean off the ground. His paws

Bird eats horse
Death comes quickly to this propalaeotherium. Not only does the gastornis crush with its beak, it also uses its powerful neck to shake the life out of the horse.

thrash in the air and for the first time he issues a long bray of panic that echoes over the lake. The gastornis tightens her grip and crushes the life out of him. Just to make sure, she bends down, pins the horse to the ground with one massive claw and delivers a series of bone-breaking bites. The whole episode is over in less than a minute. The bird pauses and looks about before tearing off a few beakfuls of meat. When she has had enough she lifts the half carcass up and carries it, swinging back and forth, back to the nest for her hatchling.

Having been hunting for a couple of hours, she is unaware of the activity of the swarm. For a moment she stands over the nest watching the ants' frantic movements. Then she drops the remains of her kill and climbs up on to the mound, furiously kicking dust and sand at the insects. Her attempts to protect her hatchling are not only too late, they are also futile. The swarm clamber on to her legs and start to bite. The thick scaly skin round her talons is impervious to the attack, but as the ants work their way up to the softer skin under her feathers the giant screeches with irritation. Her beak is not designed for grooming, but she is forced to abandon her assault on the ants and attempt to pick them out from her feathers. Eventually she has to leave the nest mound altogether. All the work that went into laying and incubating her huge egg has been wasted. She will have to start again elsewhere. The ants, meanwhile, have half a propalaeotherium to add to their trophies.

As the gastornis flees through the forest issuing her agonized rasping calls she scares the leptictidium family. The youngsters have been attempting to catch an armoured lizard, but the tough little reptile has easily repelled their advances. The extraordinary appearance of

As the ants work their way up to the softer skin under her feathers the giant screeches with irritation

Leap of faith
The leptictidium's hopping
method of locomotion allows it
to move swiftly through the
open forest understorey.

The most distinctive feature of the
leptictidium is its long flexible nose.
Covered in fine hairs, this incredibly
sensitive organ helps it to find insects
among the leaf litter on the forest floor.

the tormented gastornis sends them all bouncing off towards the lake.
The mother steers them quickly past the open silt bank and back down
one of their tracks into the undergrowth.

At the water's edge a flamingo, a rare visitor to the lake, watches the
little mammals bounce by and then goes back to grooming its feathers.
The next disturbance, however, sends it flapping up towards the
towering green curtain of the canopy. The ambulocetus has decided to
return to the bank and resume his hunting position among the sedges.
Out in the middle of the lake the second gas eruption of the day
suggests that carbon dioxide levels at the bottom are getting dangerously
high. Although the cloud quickly disperses, so many eruptions are a sign
that something much worse is on its way.

Godinotia
Several lemur-like primates were found in the Eocene forests, and some, such as *Godinotia*, had such large eye sockets that they were probably nocturnal. Their limbs show that they were adapted for leaping from one vertical tree trunk to another and then walking along the branches searching for insects.
EVIDENCE: An incomplete specimen of *Godinotia* has been found in the Messel shales.
SIZE: Body 30 centimetres (12 inches), with a long tail.
DIET: Mostly insects, but also fruit when available.
TIME: 49 million years ago.

6 p.m. The night shift takes over At sunset the sky turns a deep red streaked with orange clouds. The taller trees in the canopy pick up the pink of the last rays, while, further down, the forest floor is bathed in a blue gloom. With the lower light levels, the daylight creatures start to disappear into burrows or under bushes. The leptictidium finish their second hunting shift and once again return to the strangler fig.

As activity on the forest floor decreases, so things pick up in the trees. This is the ancient home of the mammals. During the millions of years they spent under the claw of the dinosaurs, mammals could always look for safety among the branches. Under the cloak of darkness squirrel-like ancestors evolved the type of limbs and senses needed to exploit this environment. This has stood them in good stead now the dinosaurs have gone. Many have returned to the ground, but some have stayed in the trees and become more varied and specialist. The most remarkable are the bats, which are the first creatures in the mammals' long history to evolve flight. The jungle around the lake is full of them, from the large species, with wingspans of almost 50 centimetres (18 inches), that hunt amongst the canopy, to the smaller ground hunters with wings half that size. There are also several species of primate here, another new group of arboreal specialists. They have evolved long limbs and digits, but these are for climbing trees and grasping branches.

On a thick laurel branch one such primate, a godinotia, has started his nightly search for insects and fruit. Only about 30 centimetres (12 inches) long, his fluffy black and white hair make him look quite bulky. But as he leaps from bough to bough it is clear that he is a very light, agile creature. He scans the canopy with two enormous dark eyes. Even on a moonless night he can see insects clearly and tonight he is in for a bonanza. The giant ant nest has been releasing flying males and females all day and the cnopy is full of them. Each with a wingspan of

Primates' forward facing eyes are a distinctive feature which, together with their grasping hands, allows them to thrive in the complex environment of the branches.

Night life

A godinotia watches damselflies in the moonlight. These primates are rarely found on the forest floor and are omnivorous, living mostly on insects and fruit.

51

13 centimetres (5 inches), they are a perfect meal for the godinotia and without the protection of the swarm they are easy meat.

Spotting the silvery glint of an ant's wings at the very end of a branch, the godinotia stops and weaves his head from side to side to judge the distance. Then he pounces, grasping the ant with one hand and holding on to the branch with the other hand and both feet. Besides hunting, the other activity that takes up a lot of the godinotia's time is mating. They are solitary animals, always on the look-out for members of the opposite sex. Any chance encounter and the godinotia will try to mate.

The light has not yet faded and from his vantage point the godinotia spots a predator working its way down to the lake. It is a creodont, about a metre long, a member of the mammals' first carnivorous dynasty. One day their descendants will be the giant predators of the Oligocene plains, but now

> Out of the gathering darkness a huge jaw rises up and snaps down across the front half of the creodont

they are small hunters that occasionally climb trees in search of sleepy primates. The godinotia stays very still.

Out of the gathering darkness a huge jaw rises up and snaps down across the front half of the creodont. As the smaller predator struggles, the ambulocetus swiftly reverses into the water, dragging his prey with him. Several godinotia in nearby branches screech alarm while the creodont puts up a sustained fight. But the power of the ambulocetus's bite and the length of its fangs mean that the creodont is finished once in the water. Soon the ripples and splashes die away and slowly the ambulocetus carries the limp body back to the shore to eat. After a few mouthfuls, the scent of blood in the water brings several crocodiles to the beach. They are smaller than the ambulocetus, but persistent. The rest of his meal becomes a tug of war with these reptilian rivals.

Moonlight tryst
Godinotia are fiercely solitary animals and when two adults meet there can only be one of two outcomes – they either fight or mate.

12 midnight. Death out of the darkness

Around midnight a second tremor sets off a chain of events that unleashes an indiscriminate killer into the jungle. The earthquake is followed by a huge release of gas. One end of the lake starts to boil, with water spouts erupting from the surface. Loud booms echo around the lake, accompanied by the occasional eerie flash of light. The animals in the area call and scream. Godinotia run up and down their branches in panic. Woken from her roost, even the giant gastornis squawks in alarm and then takes flight into the deeper parts of the forest. Within minutes a huge pale cloud of carbon dioxide has developed over the centre of the lake and the surface of the water has turned a sickly red as all the iron trapped in the stagnant lake suddenly oxidizes. The cloud very slowly starts to roll towards the eastern end. This is where a stream exits and, because carbon dioxide is heavier than air, it starts to flow off the lake and rolls downhill following the valley. Indeed, it is so heavy that smaller plants are crushed as it moves along. Any animal caught in its path is suffocated. On the ground, horses and pangolins perish where they sleep. Bats, birds and primates fall out of the trees. Only those in the highest branches survive. Even crocodiles and snakes on the lake shore die.

After half an hour the lake has calmed down. The red smear across its surface remains and in its eddies several bats float among the dead insects. There is a stale smell in the air, but the cloud itself has disappeared to the east. The jungle is ominously quiet, as at the eastern end of the lake every large animal for several square kilometres is dead – Nature at its most unpredictable and cruel.

Within minutes a huge pale cloud of carbon dioxide has developed over the centre of the lake and the surface of the water has turned a sickly red

Fleeing a force of nature
The forest lies on a volcanic fault and the forces
unleashed by an earthquake can send even the
mightiest predator into flight.

Perfectly preserved
It is not only animals that have been fossilized in the shales, as these delicate tea bush remains show.

Saved for posterity
Originally an iron ore site, the Messel pit was almost converted into a rubbish dump in the 1970s, before a long campaign saved it for scientific research.

Marvellous Messel

The Messel shales, near Frankfurt, Germany, are one of the most important Eocene fossil sites in the world. They were first discovered by accident in the late eighteenth century, when digging started there for iron ore and, later, brown coal. The first find was a crocodile and, despite numerous other spectacular finds, until recently fossil hunters have always had to share the site with mining companies.

The Messel shales were formed at the bottom of a deep and stagnant lake. As animals and plants fell into the lake, or drifted downstream into it, they quickly sank into the mud. Because there was very little oxygen at the bottom of the lake the usual bacteria were not present to decompose the bodies. Many remained untouched, and were preserved in every detail between the layers of mud.

Because of this unusual situation, many of the Messel's fossils show breathtaking details. Not only are leaves and insects preserved, but also the outlines of fur and feathers. This is, of course, incredibly useful in reconstructing how the animals looked. However, possibly the most amazing preservation in the Messel is of stomach contents. In many cases we can tell exactly what an animal's

last meal was. Under the microscope, the leaves in the stomachs of the small horses look just like fresh ones. The bats' too often contains the remains of their last supper – in some, small night-flying moths and caddis flies; in others, beetles. For the bats to have been hunting insects at night, they must have been using sound. Either they were very sensitive to the sound of the insects' wings in flight, or they had already developed the complex system of echolocation – making a noise and listening for the echo in order to detect where an insect was in the dark. Again, the remarkable preservation of the Messel

fossils supplies clues – the bats' ears can be X-rayed and compared with those of modern bats. This seems to show that they had not yet become echolocators, so they were not as specialized as today's bats.

In 1971, it was suggested that the pit formed at Messel should be used as a rubbish dump. Many objections were raised, and fossil hunting at the site was increased. The scientific importance of the finds eventually led to the plans being overturned, and in 1991 the site was purchased by the German government for long-term scientific use.

Sticky end (ABOVE)
This ancient relative of the woodpecker ended up at the bottom of the lake and its tail feathers are now preserved forever in stunning detail.

Strangers in the mud (LEFT)
The Messel contains many surprises, such as this relative of the hedgehog with bristles down its back and a tube of bony scales covering its tail.

Beautiful killer
In 1986 Lake Nyos was responsible for the death of over 1700 people after it released a deadly cloud of carbon dioxide.

Aftermath
The huge cloud of gas moved like an invisible avalanche downhill from the lake, choking the life out of animals and humans alike.

Lakes of death

Of all the extraordinary animals of the Messel shales, some of the most common and best preserved are the fossilized bats. This initially presented palaeontologists with a problem. Many bats looked as though they had fallen out of the air into the lake, something that modern bats simply do not do. A closer study of the geology of the lake may now have provided the answer.

On 26 August 1986 a tragedy occurred in the Cameroon Highlands of Central Africa, when a volcanic lake called Nyos suddenly released a huge volume of carbon dioxide from its deep waters. Carbon dioxide is heavier than air and a dense cloud of the gas rolled down the mountain on to several villages, suffocating everything in its path, including over 1700 people.

A study of Lake Nyos revealed a layer of oxygen-poor water at the bottom of the lake, so deep that it did not mix with the normal layers of water above it. Over the years large amounts of carbon dioxide from a volcanic spring had built up in this bottom layer. What triggered the 1986 disaster is not fully known, but something caused the two layers of water to mix and, like taking the lid off a fizzy drink bottle, all the built-up gas was suddenly released.

Coincidentally, the excellent preservation of the Messel fossils suggests that the ancient lake there must also have been very deep, with a separate layer of oxygen-poor water at the bottom. The geology of the region also indicated that 50 million years ago the Messel lake was situated on an active fault system. Geologist Bill Evans believes that siderite is an indicator of carbon-dioxide-rich lakes. Sure enough, the Messel shales also have large quantities of siderite in them.

The similarities between Lake Nyos and the Messel shales are so striking that some people think they explain all the dead bats. Periodically, large quantities of gas would escape from the lake, killing the animals on its shores and any bats that dared to swoop low over its placid waters.

The morning after
Sensing that the ambulocetus
has died, a leptictidium
inspects the corpse for
tasty insects.

6 a.m. A new day The strangler fig is positioned about halfway down the lake and as the first rays of the sun reach the forest floor it is clear that the leptictidium nest has been unaffected by the cloud. As usual, the mother leads her youngsters out at dawn down one of their trails. After about 100 metres (330 feet) they find a dead lizard on the path. Later, when they approach the lake, something much larger blocks their way. The dead body of the ambulocetus lies just inside the undergrowth where he must have dragged himself while gasping for air. Already a crocodile has crawled out of the water a few metres away and can smell the carcass. The leptictidium are at first confused. Then, when it is clear that the giant creature is not going to attack them or even move at all, the mother starts frantically to alter the direction of their path. Flicking with her powerful back legs, she has soon created a bypass through a stand of royal fern and rejoined her old track on the other side of the carcass. While she is doing this one of the youngsters has spotted prey crawling on the dead ambulocetus. He lunges and quickly eats a large ant. It would appear that the crocodiles are not the only ones interested in the ambulocetus's body.

2 Whale Killer

Our world 36 million years ago

The Earth at the end of the Eocene period is still a warm greenhouse and, at last, mammals have inherited the dinosaurs' mantle. They have started to grow in size and are now dominant on every continent. Across the northern landmasses herds of rhino-like brontotheres browse on the soft tropical vegetation and are stalked by fearsome hoofed carnivores. A few modern groups are doing well – the primates and rodents are thriving and the first elephants have appeared – but on land for the most part the ancient mammals survive. In the oceans primitive sea cows have emerged, as have the earliest giant whales. The largest creature on the planet is the 18-metre (60-foot) long basilosaurus, a worthy successor to the marine reptiles of the Mesozoic. But change is creeping across this ancient Eden. The mighty Antarctic continent has settled over the South Pole and has finally separated completely from the other continents. Surrounded by water and robbed of sun for half the year, it is undergoing a transformation. For the first time in hundreds of millions of years, there is permanent ice at the South Pole.

90 degrees east At the eastern end of the long Tethys Ocean the gap between the vast landmass of Asia to the north and the island continent of India to the south narrows to only a few kilometres. This has produced spectacular straits where towering cliffs face each other across turbulent blue waters. Although along most of the shores jungles and mangroves tumble into warm shallow waters, here the cliffs are barren – robbed of rain by the cold water currents from the south.

Off-shore, the story is completely different. The same cold currents bring clouds of nutrients, which support a massive plankton population. Shoals of fish, squid and nautiloids thrive here, feasting on the abundance of life. This in turn draws sharks and some even larger predators. Along the shores the bare rocks are blanketed in bird droppings from the flocks of seabirds that join the harvest. The straits are a marine paradise.

From the deep (PREVIOUS PAGES)
An exhausted baby dorudon just below the surface becomes easy meat for the giant whale, basilosaurus.

Ocean currents are fickle, however. Occasionally their patterns of flow change, diverting the nutrient-rich cold currents. For the plankton of the straits it is as if the annual rains have failed, producing the equivalent of a marine drought. Life in the seas is devastated. Fish that are large enough to do so move on in search of food elsewhere, but the smaller species perish in their millions. This is one such year. For once the jagged shores are mostly empty of seabirds and the water is ominously clear.

Seen from the top of the cliffs, the water is a deep dark blue and it is possible to make out the sleek light-coloured shape of a snaggletooth shark cruising close to the rocky shore. It is hunting among the many crevices for the more robust sea life that can sit out this temporary 'drought'. Despite the swell, it skirts effortlessly among the labyrinth of rocks. Invisible to the shark, but quite clearly seen from the cliff tops, its movements are being shadowed a little further out to sea by a gigantic torpedo-shaped creature. This is a basilosaurus, the largest species of whale in the Tethys, which

At home
In the late Eocene, basilosaurus is the largest animal on Earth and shows how far mammals have come since they were all small tree-dwellers during the age of the dinosaurs.

Basilosaurus

This early whale was a descendent of the terrestrial carnivores, the mesonychians. Two species are known and they were clearly common in the Eocene seas. *Basilosaurus*'s enormously long body has presented a puzzle for scientists studying its movement. The vertebrae at the end of its tail seem to be compressed, as they are in animals which have a tail fluke, but having the fluke at the end of such a long tail would make it very inefficient.

EVIDENCE: The first *Basilosaurus* fossils were found in Louisiana, but another species was soon discovered preserved in large numbers in the Fayum deposits in Egypt. Ironically many of its bones are now found in the middle of the Sahara desert.
SIZE: Females around 15 metres (50 feet) long, males around 18 metres (60 feet).
DIET: Fish, sharks, molluscs and other whales.
TIME: 40–36 million years ago.

Air force

Most of the modern bird groups, including the one containing ospreys, were established by the end of the Eocene.

Paradise lost

The late Eocene world is a paradise. After the sweltering heat of the early Eocene, the climate has changed. Instead of homogeneous heat and humidity, many parts of the world now have clearly defined dry and wet seasons, whilst the high latitudes are noticeably cooler. The tropical and subtropical continents are lined by mangrove swamps behind which are dense rainforests. In central Asia, Africa and North America the vegetation has adjusted to the new seasonal weather patterns, and vast deciduous forests have developed. The North Pole is still ice free, allowing plankton to bloom every summer, whilst a short way to the south are large regions of mixed conifer and broad-leaf forest. Some of these ecosystems have started to stabilize and will change little during the remainder of the Cenozoic.

Many species of mammal thrive in this new climate and the opening out of the forests seems to have given them the space to grow in size and number. Asia is home to the giant brontotheres, such as *Embolotherium*, and to massive carnivores such as the mesonychian *Andrewsarchus* and the bear-like creodont *Sarkastodon*. Other continents, too, have their large mammals: Africa has the early elephant *Palaeomastodon* and America its uintatheriids, giant hippo-like animals.

In the seas mighty whales such as *Basilosaurus* and *Dorudon* roam the globe from Australasia to North America, joined by a marine fauna and flora little different from today's. There are coral reefs across the globe as well as sharks, sea cows, turtles and other animals that would be recognizable in the modern world.

In North America, Europe and Asia the hoofed animals are diversifying,

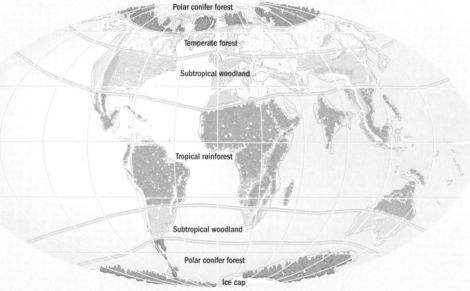

Polar conifer forest

Temperate forest

Subtropical woodland

Tropical rainforest

Subtropical woodland

Polar conifer forest

Ice cap

Cold start

Global temperatures were still high, forest still covered the continents but the first evidence of the big chill had started. Temperate forests had crept down from the poles and in the south the very first signs of an ice cap had appeared.

The Tethys was shrinking with the movement of the African continent towards Eurasia and with it dry barren areas were appearing in the tropics. South America and Australia continued north, leaving an increasingly cold antarctic behind.

Old cow
Whales are not the only mammals to have taken to the water. This period also sees the evolution of the sea cows.

Big foot
Fossil evidence from Egypt shows that the relationship between lily pad and lily trotter could be well over 30 million years old.

establishing the earliest ancestors to modern horses, rhinos and elephants. But this paradise world is about to be lost.

At the southern extreme of the globe, changes are occurring that will divert the path of evolution in the Cenozoic. As Australia and South America have moved northwards, Antarctica has become more isolated. Like a self-obsessed child, the continent's weather patterns and ocean currents have become more and more focused on itself, cutting it off from the rest of the world. Over hundreds of thousands of years this isolation has caused a negative climatic feedback which is lowering the temperature of the Antarctic continent and the seas around it. Sea ice has begun to form on its margins, causing the first icebergs to break away and drift northwards.

At the end of the Eocene the cold sea water around the Antarctic will start to move northwards. Cold water is dense, heavy and extremely mobile. Within a short period the effects will be felt as far north as Bermuda. Even the mighty Tethys Sea will show signs of fluctuating temperatures. It is like the El Niño effect on a massive scale. Tropical oceans grow cold, fish breeding patterns change and once-fertile seas become barren. On land things will

not be much better – the weather is disrupted, affecting rainfall and vegetation. It is a disaster for wildlife, much of which cannot cope with the swings of climatic change. After 30 million years of prosperity, the mammals will suffer their first ever mass extinction.

In only a few million years an estimated 20 per cent of all life on Earth will become extinct. This is not nearly as dramatic as the extinctions at the end of the Cretaceous, but it is enough to change the flow of evolution. The marine ecosystem will bear the brunt of the extinctions with fish, plankton, corals and other marine life suffering heavily under the Antarctic's icy influence. From now on the world will gradually become colder and life is going to get much tougher.

Green fringe
The Tethys was once lined with mangrove swamps. But since the movement of the African continent, their fossilized roots lie among Saharan sand dunes.

Relic from the past: one sign of basilosaurus's terrestrial ancestors is in her teeth. Her 'pierce-and-shear' fangs are very similar to those of the land-based predators the mesonychians, the group of carnivores from which the whales evolved.

makes it the biggest animal on Earth. It is also a voracious predator and every shark's nightmare.

The basilosaurus seems hardly to move her body, yet she keeps pace with the busy shark and moves a little closer. Then she drops slightly deeper. Her dark back makes her hard to spot against the sombre waters. Just as she gets to within about 30 metres (100 feet) of her quarry, the shark notices her and its tortuous hunting pattern changes into direct flight along the shoreline. The basilosaurus drives her tail down and picks up speed. As hunter and hunted sweep along the coast, she stays next to her quarry, trapping it against the rocks. After 200 metres (650 feet) the shark makes a sudden turn in an effort to escape into deeper water but, as the basilosaurus intended, it finds only the jaws of a predator. She bites twice and the snaggletooth is gone.

The basilosaurus rises to breathe. A fine spray of water explodes from her nostrils as she sucks in a lungful of air before diving and heading out towards the centre of the straits.

This female is about 15 metres (50 feet) long, mottled dark grey on top and pale grey beneath. Looking at her long elegant shape, it is hard to believe that the ancestors of a creature so beautifully adapted to water came from the land only 15 million years ago. She looks more like a giant

Maws
Rising up from below, the power of the basilosaurus's attack is enough to lift its prey clean out of the water.

Beach beasts

During the Victorian period the public assumed that sea serpents were real and the fossil finds of *Basilosaurus* seemed to confirm this scientifically.

A true sea serpent

In the early nineteenth century, sea serpents were not myths in the public imagination – they were thought to be real and people flocked to see any 'evidence' of their existence. In 1832, the American palaeontologist Dr Richard Harlan found a single backbone and identified it as belonging to a giant, extinct marine creature which he named *Basilosaurus* – 'king reptile'. Later he got hold of a jaw and noticed that it was hollow, like those of other great marine reptiles, so this confirmed his original analysis.

Good yarn

Despite there being virtually no evidence to support the existence of giant sea serpents, there continues to be famous sightings, such as this one from the 1950s off the coast of Brazil.

Shortly afterwards, a museum owner from St Louis, Missouri, found more of these bones and combined the backbones of several animals to produce a spectacular serpent-like creature almost 40 metres (130 feet) long. He took this on a highly successful tour of the United States and Europe, giving the public the evidence they craved and using Harlan's identification to support his case.

But Harlan had got it wrong. Unfortunately, he had ignored the teeth, which were of several different specialized kinds, like a mammal's, and not uniform like a reptile's. When Harlan was subsequently invited to London, the British anatomist Richard Owen examined the *Basilosaurus* jaw and teeth and declared them to belong to a mammal. He pointed out that the sperm whale had a similarly hollow jaw, and that other features of the skeleton were also very like those found in modern whales. Harlan admitted himself to be wrong, and sheepishly agreed to let Owen change the name of this strange beast to *Zeuglodon*, meaning 'yoked teeth'.

Harlan died the following year in relative obscurity, but he had the last laugh. The name he gave to the great whale lives on: in the scientific world, the first name given to an animal cannot be changed.

sea serpent than a mammal. However, her teeth – if you are unlucky enough to see them – betray her family secret. Although much larger, they are similar to the distinctive pierce-and-shear fangs of the terrestrial mesonychian predators, her distant furry cousins.

As the basilosaurus cruises further out she dives, her long, smooth form powered by the up-and-down beats of her wide tail. This is a movement unique to mammals – fish move their tails from side to side. Again it is an echo of the basilosaurus's land ancestry; the backbone she carried into the water as a mammal was adapted to flex up and down as her ancestors galloped. This new way of swimming has been evolving since the time of ambulocetus, millions of years ago.

Basilosaurus are the largest whales yet to have developed, but although this puts them at the top of the food chain, it also makes them vulnerable to the disturbance in the currents at the eastern end of the Tethys. Most have had to move away from the straits in search of food. This female is no exception and the snaggletooth was probably a welcome snack on her way west.

As the sun starts to drop towards the horizon, the southern cliffs spread shadowy fingers into the strait. The whale continues her journey, skirting along the cliffs in search of prey. Just before sunset she is harangued by a pod of dorudon. These are much smaller whales, only 5 metres (16 feet) long. They are faster swimmers than basilosaurus and too large to be eaten, but they play a dangerous game by goading the giant. She could easily injure them severely. The pod follow her for some time and then two young male dorudon swoop round and keep pace just in front of her. They cross her path repeatedly, almost as if they were trying to tease her, but the basilosaurus shows no sign of being drawn. Soon the dorudon tire of the game and melt away into the deep water to the north. The great whale continues west into the night.

Dorudon
Closely related to *Basilosaurus*, but shorter and more compact. When they were first found, in the same deposits as *Basilosaurus*, the two animals were so similar that *Dorudon* were thought to be baby *Basilosaurus*. However, real juvenile *Dorudon* have now been found, although no one has yet discovered a baby *Basilosaurus*.
EVIDENCE: Known from North America as well as from the Fayum deposits.
SIZE: 5 metres (16 feet) long.
DIET: Small fish and molluscs.
TIME: 40–36 million years ago.

Dangerous games (OVERLEAF)
A group of smaller dorudon whales harass a female basilosaurus. Although she is no danger to the adults, she will happily attack dorudon infants.

80 degrees east Almost a week after passing through the straits, the basilosaurus is approaching the middle of the northern coast of the Tethys and she is no longer alone. A large male is now escorting her and keeps a steady pace just to her right. At regular intervals they rise to the surface to breathe together, but she is not encouraging his advances. On close inspection it is clear that he is quite young. Although about 18 metres (60 feet) long, his skin shows little signs of the scarring that older males gather after years of battling. It seems that the female is probably holding out for something better.

Sure enough, as the pair approach the silt-filled waters at the mouth of an estuary, they are joined by another male. He is slightly larger and heavily scarred. For a while the younger male sticks to his position and the newcomer cruises behind as if weighing up the situation. In the end it is the female who makes the first move, turning suddenly and pulling away to the left. The older male speeds forward and cuts between the other two. He lets out a volley of bubbles and raises his tail out of the water, slapping it down in a sign of aggression. In response the younger male claps his jaw issuing underwater sounds of aggression and tries to swim round his rival. The larger whale blocks all his attempts to escort the female again and keeps up a continuous barrage of bubbles. Soon the experience and size of the older male tell and he sees the youngster off without the need for violence.

As he returns to claim his prize the female still plays hard to get. With two such large bodies floating in water, reproduction has to be a co-operative affair. The male presses his advance, trying to encourage the female to roll sideways. After an hour or so she slows and allows him to draw nearer. She drifts to the surface and finally rolls on her side. As he pushes himself against her, an extraordinary legacy of their land ancestry appears. To help guide his penis, two tiny limbs flip out from his body to grasp a matching pair on her. After millions of years of marine evolution

Synchronized swimming
Basilosaurus's long serpentine shapes make mating underwater difficult. They have retained their back limbs to help hold their bodies close together.

these diminutive organs are all that is left of the whales' hind limbs. Their only role now is to assist in mating.

The coupling is brief, but it is the first of many. The old male will now escort the female for days, not only to mate again but also to prevent other males usurping his position.

During this time it is likely that the female will continue to travel westwards. The middle of the Tethys has not been affected by the erratic cold currents that forced her to leave the eastern straits. However, the waters to the west are richer in food, and if she is going to sustain a pregnancy she will need to seek the best hunting grounds. The shoreline here is very different from the bare, craggy cliffs to the east. Shallow corals border long sandy beaches and extensive dune systems. It is the same for hundreds of kilometres, broken only occasionally by estuaries where the silt carried by the rivers has cut through the coral barriers. Behind the dunes poor soil conditions have created a low-growing tropical shrub habitat, which is more open than most parts of the continent. The mammals that thrive among the palms and yucca are larger than their forest counterparts; some even approach the size of the long-extinct dinosaurs.

In the shade of a tall yucca grove, a herd of brontotheres sit out the heat of the midday sun. These are some of the biggest herbivores on Earth. The largest males can be almost 3 metres (10 feet) at the shoulder and weigh well over a tonne. The males also sport the large heart-shaped nose horn so distinctive of this species. Members of the herd sit or stand in the shade, gently chewing over the last of their morning's browsing. Necklaces of saliva hang from their broad muzzles and hordes of flies crowd round their eyes. Their tough hides are caked in the pale mud of the area, which helps to keep them cool and holds off some of the insects. Small birds hop over their bodies searching for parasites. Some also drink at their nostrils or pick at their ear wax – an activity that the brontotheres seem hardly to notice.

Male

Female

Brontotheres

A group of animals which at this time was common and widespread. They are related to the rhinos, tapirs and horses and are well-adapted to more open environments, probably browsing in huge herds across Asia and America.

EVIDENCE: Brontotheres are found in several deposits in Mongolia, and also in huge numbers in the state of Wyoming.

SIZE: About 2.5 metres (8 feet) high at the shoulder.

DIET: Browsed the lower branches of trees, shrubs and other soft, easily digested vegetation.

TIME: 55–30 million years ago.

Face-off

Two gigantic brontotheres size each other up.
These confrontations rarely come to blows
since males tend to be very good judges
of size and know when to back off.

Although the fully grown adults are too large to fear local predators, the herd usually stick together to protect their young. Today, however, one female stands alone among the scrub and cacti, a little apart from the herd. At her feet lies the reason – a stillborn baby. Although she gave birth during the night she apparently still cannot understand why her offspring does not get up. Trapped by her maternal instincts, she stands over the corpse, occasionally dipping her head and nudging it.

After waiting patiently for hours she suddenly becomes agitated, calling out and stomping her feet. It soon becomes clear why. Slinking through the shrubs comes an andrewsarchus, a huge scavenger that probably smelt the corpse kilometres away. Andrewsarchus is, by some way, the largest member of a group of carnivores called the mesonychians. They are distantly related to whales and, surprisingly, are ungulates, which means that they have hooves instead of claws. This suits the andrewsarchus's scavenging lifestyle because it helps him to cover large distances in search of food. He also has enormous jaws, almost a metre long, which are mostly used for crushing bones and chasing other creatures off kills.

As he trots towards the mother brontothere, he raises his dark brown hackles, and snaps and grinds his teeth to intimidate her. But she is not about to abandon her young so easily. As soon as her small eyes spot the scavenger she charges, snorting and bucking her head. Wisely, the andrewsarchus gallops to one side, putting a knot of yucca between him and the enraged mother. She returns to her baby and, more urgently now, pushes at the corpse, trying to hook it on her horn so that she can carry it away from danger. But despite her best efforts they both remain in the open.

Throughout the long hot afternoon there is a stand-off. The andrewsarchus keeps probing the mother's resolve and gradually she begins to lose interest in defending her dead calf. Each time she chases the

Andrewsarchus
The largest of a group of carnivores, the mesonychians, which are closely related to the hoofed herbivores. Although *Andrewsarchus* is known from only one skull, the skull is characteristic of the group. Mesonychian fossils are usually found alone and around water, and this attachment to water eventually led to one group of mesonychians becoming entirely marine – the whales.
EVIDENCE: Mesonychians are found in Asia, Europe and America, with the *Andrewsarchus* skull being discovered in Mongolia.
SIZE: The skull found in Mongolia is about 83 centimetres (33 inches) long, which would make *Andrewsarchus* about 1.9 metres (6 feet 3 inches) high and 5 metres (16 feet) long – the largest meat-eating land mammal ever.
DIET: Probably scavenged along the water's edge, perhaps using their huge jaws to crush turtles and catch small crocodiles.
TIME: 60–32 million years ago.

High noon
A female brontothere automatically defends her baby from the attentions of an andrewsarchus, even though the youngster is stillborn.

Decorative feature: all brontotheres sport horns of various shapes and sizes, but because they are made of brittle bone they are not as useful in fights as it would appear. Any damage is extremely painful for the animal.

First come, first served
Two andrewsarchus squabble over an abandoned baby brontothere. At a kill, these scavengers yield to nothing, except possibly another andrewsarchus.

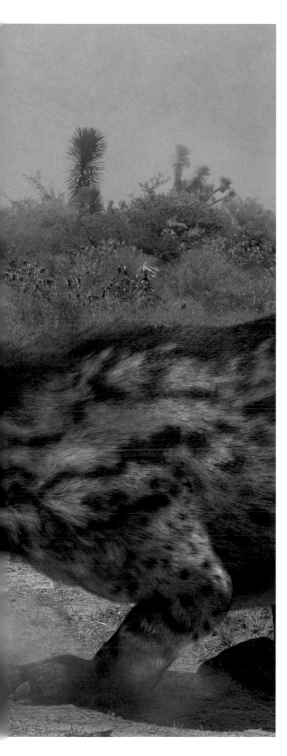

scavenger away she returns to the body a little more slowly. By early evening a second andrewsarchus has appeared and this seems to finish the affair. After one bellowing charge the brontothere does not return to the corpse – instead she stands blinking as if she had forgotten what she was doing. The two scavengers pounce on the carcass, snarling and snapping. A tug-of-war develops as each tries to wrestle the entire prize for himself.

In a bizarre twist, the sight of her calf bouncing about between the scavengers seems to make the mother brontothere think it is alive and once again she charges to its rescue. This time she catches the first andrewsarchus squarely on the pelvis, sending it writhing in agony across the dusty ground. As he struggles to escape she keeps after him, eventually losing sight of him in the tall shrubs. Sadly, all her intervention really achieves is to give the carcass to the other scavenger. While the mother is occupied, he uses his strong neck and powerful jaws to lift the calf and carry it off into the dunes. Eventually he settles down on the beach and starts to eat.

All-purpose: andrewsarchus has many adaptations to help it deal with its varied diet. Chief among these are its huge jaws that can tear, pierce, rip or crush almost any carcass which it finds.

Distant echo
Many have likened *Andrewsarchus*'s lifestyle to that of a hyena. Certainly there are similarities in the crushing power of the jaws, although *Andrewsarchus* was probably four times as big.

A sheep in wolf's clothing

It may look like a gigantic dog but *Andrewsarchus* is in fact one of the most bizarre mammals ever to have evolved. At 5 metres (16 feet) long it is the largest known mammalian land carnivore, yet it is an ungulate: this means it is more sheep than wolf.

Everything we know about *Andrewsarchus* comes from a single skull specimen recovered during one of Roy Chapman Andrews' Mongolian palaeontology expeditions in the 1920s (see *Treasure hunters in the Gobi,* pages 130–1), the animal being named in honour of Andrews himself. This skull is truly enormous, measuring 83 centimetres (33 inches) in length and fortunately it contains teeth, which means we can guess at its lifestyle.

At first palaeontologists thought the skull might belong to some kind of giant pig. It has a long, narrow jaw, like that of a wolf or dog, and its teeth are very varied – sharp and fang-like at the front, but broad and blunt at the back. To scientists this suggested that *Andrewsarchus* was probably capable of eating a range of foods. It could use its front fangs for gripping and tearing meat, whilst its back molars could crush and grind bone, shell or maybe even nuts and roots. In other

words, *Andrewsarchus* could probably have eaten just about anything it came across. A close examination of individual teeth revealed that they were chipped and broken, suggesting that whatever *Andrewsarchus* was eating was very tough indeed. But far from confirming that it was a pig, these teeth actually placed it in a group of carnivores called the mesonychians. The limbs of the mesonychians, although strong, were not built for speed and, most crucially of all, these animals had no claws to kill large prey. Instead they had a small hoof on the end of each toe, which is the tell-tale sign that relates them to today's hoofed animals such as horses and sheep. Based on this evidence, most scientists now think that the mesonychians, including *Andrewsarchus*, were scavengers.

Fearsome fossil
All that scientists have of this creature is one skull found by Chapman Andrews in Mongolia – but it is a remarkable object.

By now it is late in the day and the wind off the sea drives the sand across the beach in a low, stinging layer. The andrewsarchus keeps his eyes half closed and dips his head to the task of finishing off a very sandy carcass. About 20 metres (65 feet) in front of him a large dome appears in the surf and glistens in the evening light. Soon it is followed by another further down the beach, and another.

This is a loggerhead turtle laying beach, and by nightfall the andrewsarchus is snarling and snapping at the hundreds of lumbering turtles making their way up the beach to lay their eggs. They are fortunate because the andrewsarchus normally likes nothing better than to raid turtle nests and even use its massive jaws to crush smaller species. But tonight the scavenger has eaten his fill and the turtles are no more than a nuisance. Eventually he abandons what is left of the carcass and heads off into the night, probably noting the beach so that when he is next hungry he can return to dig up some eggs.

The laying goes on all night, with each female taking several hours to complete the exhausting task of crawling up the beach, digging a hole, laying, filling the hole in and returning to the sea. By dawn there are several hundred tired turtles returning to the safety of deeper water to feed and rest. But this is when the basilosaurus strikes. She rises from below and clamps her jaws over a turtle's flipper. It struggles briefly and then departs – without its flipper. The shell of the loggerhead is too thick even for the basilosaurus, but she is quite happy to take her prey apart bit by bit. The reptiles can do little to stop her except head for the sea floor and hope she moves on. Ultimately, though, these are only snacks for the whale – the turtles do not delay her journey west for long. With her back to the rising sun, she abandons her hunt. She is still being shadowed by her huge mate, but soon he will abandon her in search of other females and she will be left to give birth and to raise her calf alone.

Belly up
Turtles can rely on their shells to resist most attacks, but they are no defence against an andrewsarchus's crushing jaws.

35 degrees east As the weeks pass the basilosaurus finds herself in the shallower, warm waters of the western Tethys. These ancient waterways have been full of marine life since the time of the dinosaurs and food is plentiful for the giant whale. Mostly she hunts in deeper water as she is too long to pick her way among the vast coral barriers that fringe the coast. But occasionally she gets a chance to change her diet.

Just off the north coast of Africa she is drawn into a deep-water channel that leads through a gap in the coral. This is kept open by the choking silt from a large estuary beyond. Floating upside down in the grey-blue water is the bloated carcass of a brontothere, probably carried from many kilometres inland by the river. Sharks, with their almost uncanny ability to find carrion in the water, are there already and the body jolts from repeated attacks. The basilosaurus begins to circle. But a few metres below the small predators are two isurus. These are big sharks, ancestors of the great whites, and they are more than a match for basilosaurus.

These ancient waterways have been full of marine life since the time of the dinosaurs and food is plentiful for the giant whale

As the basilosaurus holds back, the sharks attack again and again, and the carcass starts to disintegrate. Chased by a silvery blizzard of smaller scavengers, its head drifts to the muddy bottom. Soon the whole animal will sink and what is left will become hagfish fodder. A third isurus appears and the basilosaurus decides to move on without taking a bite. There are other smells and tastes here that might give her an easier meal, such as apidium.

The estuary forms a huge bay with numerous deep channels. As she explores these she passes over fields of lush sea grass, above which float the unmistakable rotund shapes of sea cows. Like the whale, these were, until comparatively recently, furry land mammals, but have been drawn back into the marine environment by the promise of easy food. Unlike the whale it

Fruits of the forest
The forests around the Tethys are a rich source of fruits and the primate apidium is just one of the species that has evolved to exploit this.

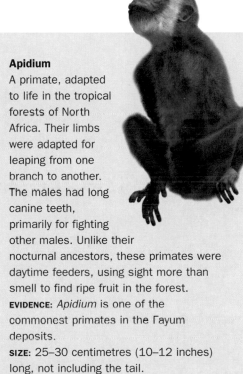

Apidium
A primate, adapted to life in the tropical forests of North Africa. Their limbs were adapted for leaping from one branch to another. The males had long canine teeth, primarily for fighting other males. Unlike their nocturnal ancestors, these primates were daytime feeders, using sight more than smell to find ripe fruit in the forest.
EVIDENCE: *Apidium* is one of the commonest primates in the Fayum deposits.
SIZE: 25–30 centimetres (10–12 inches) long, not including the tail.
DIET: Fruit.
TIME: 36–34 million years ago.

wasn't meat they were after but the sea grass which is so abundant in these sunlit waters. These slow, gentle creatures are too large to be threatened by predators, even basilosaurus, although it is fortunate that they happen to have no young with them. The whale carries on towards the coast.

In front of her stretches the Fayum coast, with some of the richest and most varied stands of tropical jungle in the world. Bordering the sea are

dense mangrove swamps, but just behind them lie kilometre upon kilometre of ancient forest, full of tall trees with massive root buttresses. Pawpaw, ylang ylang, cashews, obeche and fan palms are just some of the bewildering variety that grow here and the many freshwater channels are lined with cat's tail and choked with floating fern. Most of the trees here bear fruit and are rich in oils and resin. Consequently, the evening air is full of pungent fragrances and the howls of troops of apidium monkeys moving through the canopy looking for trees whose fruit is ripe.

Like most primates, apidium are at home in the trees, the ancient sanctuary of all mammals. Since these trees fruit all year round there is always food to be found somewhere and the monkeys are experts at foraging through the canopy. However, this forest is also divided by numerous rivers which the troops frequently face the task of crossing. They leap if they can, but often they have to swim and that is what the aquatic predators are waiting for.

As the basilosaurus approaches the shallows, one troop is negotiating a channel lined with mangroves. It is too wide to be leapt, but a bunch of roots protruding from one side allows the more agile members to jump and then scrabble across, hardly getting their feet wet. For the mothers carrying babies and for the older animals, this is more of a challenge. Most leap just short and, after a thorough soaking, drag themselves out. But the fifth to do this drops into the water. There is a flurry of splashes and he fails to resurface. The troop shake the branches and howl at each other across the dangerous channel. Blood appears in the water and a grey fin cuts the surface – the apidium has been killed by a shark. These predators take a heavy toll of monkeys in these salty waters and if the apidium move away from the coast crocodiles perform the same function in fresh water. The troop gradually calm down, but it is a long while before the next monkey attempts to cross.

Leap of faith
In order to seek out fruit trees
in the swamps, the apidium
have to cross waterways.
There are plenty of predators
to take advantage of those
that do not make it.

All hands and feet: the exceptional hand-eye
co-ordination of the primates, which helps
them leap from branch to branch, sets them
apart from other forest animals.

The secret Sahara
These strange rocks in the Sahara are fossilized mangrove roots and stand as testament to the area's lush past.

The fabulous Fayum

There is perhaps no better example of the effects of climate and geology change over time than the discovery of mangrove fossils in the middle of the Sahara Desert. The secret lush past of this great desert was first uncovered in a region of northern Egypt called the Fayum Depression. In the mid-nineteenth century scientists found not only fossilized trees and mangrove swamps, but ancient whale bones eroding out of the sand dunes. It was clear that 36 million years ago this was a stunningly rich habitat. Early whales shared the warm shallow waters with sea cows and hippo-like *Moeritherium*. Fishing eagles hunted above the water, and the channels were clothed with water lilies, providing a pontoon for giant lily-trotters to walk

Early whales shared the warm shallow waters with sea cows and hippo-like *Moeritherium*. Fishing eagles hunted above the water, and the channels were clothed with water lilies

across. The tropical trees above were filled with primates and marsupials, and the ground below stalked by ancient carnivorous creodonts and giant rhinoceros-like arsinotheres. The site was an irresistible draw for fossil hunters.

Ancient ancestors
For the first time in the Fayum, scientists found the ancestral elephants – and there were already several different types. The skull above belonged to one called *Phiomia*.

In 1907, an expedition was sent from the American Museum of Natural History, New York, to the Fayum. This was the first time American palaeontologists had left their shores in search of fossil material, and the president himself, Theodore Roosevelt, wrote a letter of introduction for them to carry. The evocative diaries of the expedition leader, Walter Granger, describe the trouble they had with the poor preservation of the fossils. Whilst there, he was given a fossil which was to prove the Fayum had extra-special importance for the history of mankind. It was a simple left lower jaw, and when returned to the US it was misidentified as being from some sort of hoofed animal and named *Apidium*, meaning 'little bull'. It turned out to be the remains of a primate and, after a gap of 40 years, the potential of the Fayum for the study of our earliest ancestors was realized.

In the 1950s, a researcher at Oxford University, Elwyn Simons, started work on these early primates and began to review the known Fayum fossils, showing that they covered crucial periods in primate evolution. In the 1980s, expeditions also started to study the early whales more closely. Both primates and whales continue to be excavated and studied, and the Fayum has turned out to be one of the most important fossil sites in the world for understanding the early evolution of some of today's most familiar mammals.

Diverse giants
During their evolution there have been several different major groups of elephants, like the gomphotheres (above), mastodons and mammoths.

Americans abroad
The 1907 American Natural History Museum's expedition to the Fayum was the first time American palaeontologists had left their own shores in search of fossils.

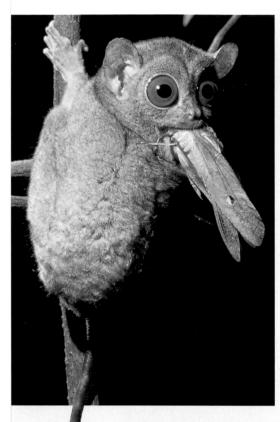

Our ancestors' ancestors

Trying to identify the very first primates among all the other tree-dwelling mammals of the early Cenozoic is not easy. Very little separates our early ancestors from those of rats or squirrels. But when in doubt palaeontologists look at the teeth and this has focused them on group of squirrel-like mammals known as plesiadapiforms. These seem to have been very common in the Palaeocene, coming in a number of sizes and eating a range of foods. Most appear to have lived in the trees, feeding on insects, fruit, vegetation or seeds. Some may even have fed on gum seeping from tree trunks like modern marmosets. It is the pattern and shape of their teeth that apparently places them at the head of the primate family.

In the Eocene period, though, the first definite primates appear – the prosimians. Unlike the plesiadapiforms, these early prosimians showed many of the characteristics recognizable in modern primates. Instead of claws, they had flat nails; their snouts were shorter and their eyes more forward-facing; their legs were longer and slimmer, and on their hind feet the big toe was opposable to the rest. They relied on their eyes more than on their nose or whiskers to find their way around. The prosimians were as successful as the plesiadapiforms had been, and split into two main groups, the big-eyed, leaping omomyids (looking like modern tarsiers) – and the lemur-like adapids (such as those found in the Messel deposits mentioned in Chapter 1).

The Fayum primates span the boundary between Eocene and Oligocene. Alongside the prosimians appeared the first 'higher primates', including *Apidium*. These animals were beginning to look 'monkey-like', although they still had a lot of prosimian features, and it was from this kind of animal that the familiar monkeys and apes – including ourselves – would later evolve.

Monkey's uncle
The prosimians are a very ancient group of primates whose living survivors include the modern tarsiers (above) and lemurs.

Familiar face
Higher primates did not evolve until the end of the Eocene, but by then they would have been recognizable as monkeys, similar to this howler monkey.

The basilosaurus herself is far too large to join in a monkey hunt. Instead she cruises the sea-grass beds looking for small sharks. However, today offers something a little different. Among the mangroves several moeritherium are paddling through shallows, grazing on vegetation both above and below the waterline. Less than a metre high, these enchanting hippo-like creatures are in fact an early type of elephant. Their noses are clear evidence for this, they droop over their mouths, making them look like sad old men. Despite appearances, these extended noses make them very efficient at gathering vegetation underwater without using their limbs. Some of moeritherium's distant relatives have already taken this clever little adaptation and evolved it into a trunk – an organ so good at gathering food that it will found a whole dynasty of mammal giants such as mastodons, elephants and mammoths.

One of these little pink animals has waddled out on a sand bar at low tide to graze on some exposed seaweed. Now the tide has returned he is

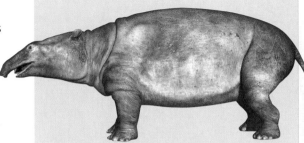

Moeritherium
By the end of the Eocene, there were already several members of the elephant family, some of them very similar in appearance to modern elephants. *Moeritherium*, however, was a side branch which seems to have adopted a hippo-like lifestyle.
EVIDENCE: The first fossils were discovered in the Fayum in 1904, but it has since been found in other sites around North and West Africa.
SIZE: 0.7 metres (2 feet 4 inches) at the shoulder.
DIET: Sea grass and other floating/waterside vegetation.
TIME: 36–33 million years ago.

Taking a breather
The swampy conditions at the edges of the Tethys are ideal for creatures such as the moeritherium, which are as at home in water as they are on land.

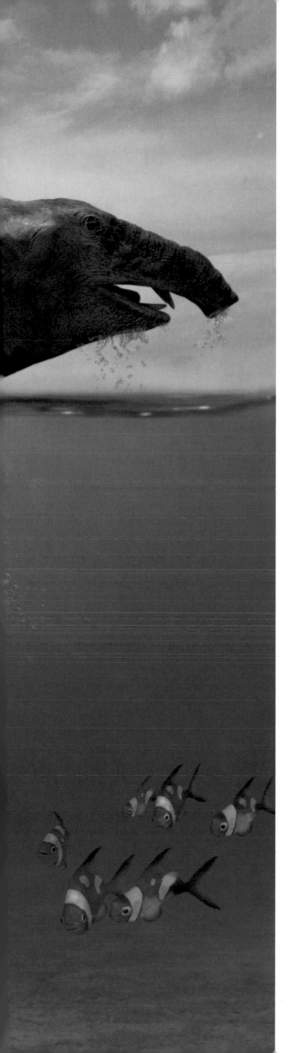

Shape of things to come: the distinctive long nose and tusks of the moeritherium were so useful that its distant relatives – the elephants – exploited them in many shapes and forms.

cut off from the mangroves by a channel of fast-moving water. After a short while, honking in distress at the other moeritherium on the bank opposite, he plops into the water and starts to swim for his life against the tide. The basilosaurus has heard the commotion and smells the chubby herbivore. She closes on the tidal channel. Unaware of the danger he is in, the moeritherium is making slow progress, his thrashing short legs only just keeping him from being swept away.

The basilosaurus soon has sight of her prey and, after a moment's pause, heads straight for him. As the moeritherium's nose quivers skywards to suck in yet another lungful of air, the water around him explodes and he is thrown sideways. Miraculously he is unhurt and is soon desperately continuing his struggle towards the mangroves. In her haste, the huge whale has grounded herself on the bar just short of her victim. Two thirds of her length now lolls on the sand with a tidal swell running past her. Her body is so long that, although she thrashes her powerful tail, the last third in the water is not enough to pull her back.

Eventually, the moeritherium reaches the mangroves and stumbles out among the aerial roots. Once safe among the branches he looks back with his long snout twitching. Some 30 metres (100 feet) away the whale's

Swimming for it
Moeritherium rarely venture out into deeper water, but, if forced, are powerful swimmers despite their ponderous shape.

Close call

A moeritherium, stranded by the tide on a sandbank, gets far closer to marine life than he intended. Fortunately for the herbivore the basilosaurus is temporarily stranded in the attack and the moeritherium manages to escape.

whole body is convulsing as it tries to move back into deeper water. Not only that, but with each convulsion the current is dragging her further on to the sand. The moeritherium turns and runs off, crashing through the swamp.

The basilosaurus is in trouble – she cannot free herself. But luck is with her. When she attacked the moeritherium the tide was not completely in and still had 30 centimetres (12 inches) more to rise. This in itself is not enough to free her but, after an hour, the tide turns and the current drags her back out to sea again. After being stranded for two and half hours the basilosaurus finally escapes and heads straight out of the bay – exhausted, but alive.

After being stranded for two and half hours the basilosaurus finally escapes and heads straight out of the bay – exhausted, but alive

30 degrees east It is now just under a year since the basilosaurus mated and she has spent most of that time in the western Tethys, plucking life from the coral walls. With such a large foetus inside her she needs to keep herself well fed – any prolonged period of starvation and she will spontaneously abort. Like any potential mother she also has to keep herself as fit and healthy as possible in preparation for the trial ahead. This includes the apparently bizarre behaviour of rubbing herself along the seabed. Whales may be the most feared predators in the oceans, but to marine parasites they are just big soft targets and a range of unpleasant animals make their home in and on the basilosaurus's skin. Shedding layers of skin helps her control parasites such as lice and barnacles.

The female dives to the bottom, about 10 metres (30 feet) down. The sea floor is thick with nummulitids – shelled plankton the size of coins. These are incredibly successful creatures in the Eocene Tethys, covering vast areas of the seabed. Each disc is made by one single-celled animal which over a

Safe distance
Once back on dry land the moeritherium can safely ponder the plight of the giant whale that almost had him for lunch.

Valley of the king lizards

Stone whales
Philip Gingerich excavates whale fossils in the Egyptian valley that may once have seen the slaughter of infant dorudon by the carnivorous *Basilosaurus*.

Tethys tyrant
Looking at the skull of *Basilosaurus*, even a non-expert can see how the whale gained its fearsome reputation.

Although Egypt is better known for the Valley of the Kings, it also has a valley of the whales located in the desert just outside Cairo. Here the fossils of *Basilosaurus* and *Dorudon* are concentrated in one area: literally hundreds of them are eroding out of the desert rocks. The Zeuglodon Valley, as it is known, is part of the Fayum fossil beds and has always presented scientists with a puzzle – why so many in one place? Other fossils in the Zeuglodon Valley include sharks, crocodiles and *Moeritherium*, which makes experts think that the area may once have been a quiet estuary or a sheltered bay. It has been suggested that the whales became lost and stranded themselves in the shallow water, as modern whales sometimes do, but the fossil skeletons are too complete for this to be likely and do not show the characteristic

signs of sun-bleaching that modern stranded whales have.

More clues came as the result of an intensive study by Professor Philip Gingerich, one of the world's leading fossil whale experts. He noticed that all the *Basilosaurus* skeletons were from adults, whilst there were both *Dorudon* adult and baby specimens. Furthermore, many of the juvenile *Dorudon* showed signs of having been attacked by a predator large enough to crush their skulls. Only one known predator from the time was powerful enough to do this – *Basilosaurus*. Gingerich suggested that the *Dorudon* had come into the bay to give birth, only to find themselves attacked by *Basilosaurus*.

Gingerich also discovered another fascinating detail about *Basilosaurus* in Zeuglodon Valley – how they mated. Until his work, it had always been assumed that *Basilosaurus* had lost its back legs. But careful excavation was rewarded when Gingerich found two tiny but perfectly formed legs in place at the back of a giant *Basilosaurus* skeleton. He could only conclude that these vestigial limbs were still there because they performed an important role during mating, possibly grasping hold of the mate's genitalia, just as crocodiles do with their claspers.

period of years has built a spiral shell. Some can grow to several centimetres wide and live for up to a hundred years. Compared with other single-celled creatures, most of which are not visible to the naked eye, nummulitids are gigantic. Here they carpet the seafloor, lying several metres thick.

The whale curves her long body and in the dim blue light drags herself through the nummulitids, sending clouds of debris up into the water. By the time she has finished, fine sheets of her skin hang in the water like net curtains. A few parasites will have been dislodged, but keeping herself clean is a life sentence.

As her time draws near she needs food and, as luck would have it, she is about to be offered it on a plate. Her wanderings once again take her closer to the coast. Just beyond the coral there is a wide, shallow bay where every year pods of dorudon seek out the warm, still waters to give birth. There are several thousand small whales in the bay and, by now, several hundred babies too. The buff-coloured youngsters ride close to their mothers, as most are not strong enough to swim for any distance. At regular intervals each one is gently coaxed to the surface to breathe because they also cannot hold their breath for long. All this makes them very vulnerable to predators for the first few days.

It could be that the basilosaurus has been here before or that she is following the scent of the birthing dorudon, but she easily manages to navigate her way through the coral into the bay. Adult dorudon are quite capable of an aggressive defence, even against the basilosaurus. As she slips into the bay several females start to harass her – swimming close and snapping or tail-slapping in front of her. However, the basilosaurus ignores these threats and starts to cruise round the bay. The mothers and young become agitated and are forced to keep on the move to avoid the predator. Occasionally she heads straight for the pods, there is a flurry of panic and snapping, and then she returns to the outer part of the bay.

Whale housekeeping
A basilosaurus scrapes herself along the sea floor to remove layers of skin and with them many of the parasites that regularly plague the whale.

After about half an hour her plan pays off. The newborn are exhausted and are finding it increasingly difficult to keep up with their mothers. On her next attack run, the basilosaurus almost bumps into a baby stranded by its fleeing mother. Before an adult can come to its aid the baby is gone and a long trail of blood swirls after the basilosaurus as she returns to the deeper waters of the outer bay. Unfortunately for the dorudon the assault is not over. Before the afternoon is out she will have taken two more calves and several more will have drowned, too tired to rise to the surface and breathe. Through the death of these babies the basilosaurus ensures the success of her own.

In mother's shadow
Newborn whales tire very quickly, which makes them vulnerable to attack. As a result this young dorudon needs constant protection from his mother.

10 degrees west At the very western end of the Tethys, the basilosaurus stops to give birth. This is the edge of her world. For a while she drifts near the surface, her body arched with contractions. Suddenly a long, snake-like baby slips, nose first, into the ocean. The mother guides her infant up for its first breath of air with her snout – the ruthless killer turns gentle mother.

The Tethys has been the cradle of the whales' rapid evolution, but this stable, warm environment is slowly changing. The movement of the continents is squeezing

Cold currents from the south are causing changes in water temperature. The era of ancient whales such as basilosaurus is coming to an end

the old sea, and cold currents from the south are causing changes in water temperature. The era of ancient whales such as basilosaurus is coming to an end. Far to the south other species are evolving to conquer even the deepest, coldest ocean. These waters are rich in plankton and the whales have specially adapted to harvest it. One day their descendants – the filter-feeding baleen whales, such as the blue whale – will become the largest animals ever to grace the planet.

Our world 24 million years ago

After the long and drawn-out upheavals of the transition from the Eocene to the Oligocene, the climate appears to have settled and global temperatures are stable. Sea levels are lower and the polar forests to the south have disappeared, as have the vast tropical forests that once stretched up into high latitudes. Instead, wide belts of broad-leaved deciduous woodland separate the tropics from the poles. But this apparently quiet time hides a slow revolution amongst plants. The dark green grip of the Eocene forests has been broken. Herbs, shrubs and annuals are enjoying their moment in the sun and, for the first time, there appears a group of plants that will eventually dominate vast areas of the Earth – the grasses. The endless open woodland of eastern Asia have created some truly monstrous animals. The gigantic indricotheres are the largest land mammals ever to have existed. The Earth has not seen their like since the time of the dinosaurs.

Size matters (PREVIOUS PAGES) Indricotheres are gentle herbivores and their young are utterly dependent when born. But with a mature male weighing in at almost 15 tonnes, their sheer size makes the adults almost invincible.

The newcomer A huge yellow moon rises over the open floodplains of Hsanda Gol. Gnarled old oaks throw night-time shadows across the low scrub and, above the drone of insects, a family of bear dogs call to each other in the silvery light. Here and there across the plains seasonal rivers have cut into the soft earth, creating long, low bluffs, and at the base of one of these lies the carcass of a small rhino-like hyracodon. It is a recent kill, probably brought down in the late evening; whoever the predators were they have moved on, leaving just the larger bones behind.

Trotting through the saltbush comes the unmistakable bulk of a huge male hyaenodon. These magnificent predators thrive here on the plains, but worldwide their kind is in decline. The group they belong to, the creodonts, used to be the dominant mammalian predators, but now the hyaenodons are one of the few types left. New, faster groups of predators, such as the Carnivora, are taking over.

Periodically the hyaenodon stops and sniffs the air, trying to track down the source of the smell he picked up about a kilometre away. As he draws close to the bluff he becomes more cautious. He is clearly very old. His coat is patchy and, as well as several old scars, he carries a deep fresh wound across the bridge of his snout. Despite his size there are numerous creatures on these plains that could chase him from a kill. Luckily for him, it looks as if he has what is left of the hyracodon to himself. He growls at a couple of small bear dogs prowling nearby and settles down to feed.

He starts to chew on a femur but, in another sign of old age, he has trouble. Hyaenodons have massively powerful jaws, but every time they open and shut them they grind the back teeth together. This constant shearing wears the teeth down and, after a certain age, they lose the ability to chew. If an old hyaenodon doesn't die a violent death, it usually starves because its teeth are no longer working properly.

Hyaenodons

These were very successful predators from a group known as creodonts. In the Hsanda Gol, four or more species have been found. The smaller species would have been the lions of the Mongolian plains – hunting in packs, most often at night, and using their powerful jaws to crush bones – whilst the largest would probably have hunted alone. The males show grinding marks on their teeth very like modern animals which use the noise of grinding teeth as an intimidation display.

EVIDENCE: *Hyaenodon* fossils are common in the Hsanda Gol formation, and are also found in North America.

SIZE: 30 centimetres–1.7 metres (1 foot– 6 feet 6 inches) at the shoulder.

DIET: These were the prime hunters of the plains, designed for fast running, and only rivalled at the kill by giant, scavenging entelodonts.

TIME: 41–24 million years ago.

Oligocene stand-off
Hyaenodons are the most powerful predators on the plains but this mother and her cubs are the ones in danger when faced by an irritated indricothere.

Out in the open

New horizons
After being covered in tropical forest, during the Oligocene the landscape began to open out.

The Oligocene epoch lasted from 35 to 23 million years ago. It is a crucial period because it links the archaic world of the tropical Eocene and the more modern-looking ecosystems of the Miocene. At the beginning the climate was much colder and drier than the Eocene and many animals had trouble adapting to these conditions. Early casualties included the basilosaurid whales and the carnivorous mesonychians, both of which became extinct.

As the epoch progresses, the first of the more modern herbivores begin to appear. The plains of Asia, North America and Europe fill up with new species of horse, deer, camels, tapirs, brontotheres and indricotheres. These new mammals are much larger than their archaic ancestors. They are lean and long-legged with specialized feet and a reduced number of toes so that they can walk long distances efficiently and move at speed if necessary. Size and mobility help them cope with more extreme seasons. Their teeth, too, are evolving so that they can expand their diet to include the wider range of plants that are becoming available to them.

These new shapes reflect what is happening to the vegetation. Whereas the Eocene world was dominated by dense rainforests up to the poles, the cooler and drier Oligocene is characterized by the spread of broad-leaved deciduous woodlands and open plains. The Eocene rainforests did not have room for herds of large indricotheres. However, there is still not enough grass about to make the plains look anything like a modern savannah. In fact, grass is not on the menu at all – most herbivores are browsers, chewing on leaves, vines, roots and fruit.

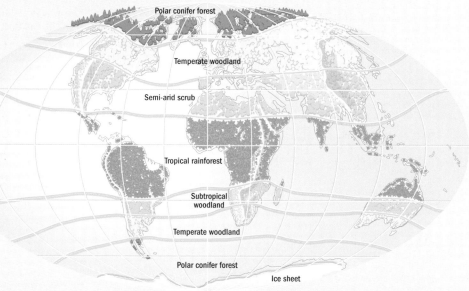

Forest retreat
The lonely Antarctic was now turning into the familiar frozen wilderness we know today. A permanent ice sheet had developed and cold currents were spreading out across the ocean. The ancient Tethys sea had all but disappeared and the modern bands of tropical, sub-tropical temperature and polar vegetation had started to appear. Forests were still the order of the day, but more open woodlands and desert areas led to the evolution of giant land mammals.

Run rabbit
Oligocene rabbits did not have the long ears of their modern descendants, nor their jumping back legs, but they did probably enjoy grass.

A new breed of leaner and faster herbivores presents a challenge to the predators of the Oligocene. This is bad news for the large archaic carnivores, such as the creodonts which are heavily built and cumbersome animals, capable of feeding only on slower game. As horses, camels, rhinos and others have become more specialized, it has taken a new breed of carnivore to catch up with them.

The first members of the order Carnivora appear about now. Today this group dominates the large predator classes, but among their first attempts at a hunting mammal is the small cat-like *Nimravus*, which prowls the plains of Asia

and North America. Also there are the bear dogs, a light, fast-moving group of predators that concentrate on small mammals. In the future they will evolve into bear-sized giants capable of bringing down very large prey.

Although the role of Antarctica is pivotal at this time, not all the events of the Oligocene can be blamed on the cooling climate. Some are a function of changes in the physical world. In North America the uplift of the Rocky Mountains modifies the continental climate, whilst the periodic raising and lowering of sea levels allow

The Oligocene is far from being a quiet time. In many ways it is laying the foundations of the world we live in today

many large animals to cross between the North American and Eurasian continents. This has led to a cosmopolitan mixture of creatures across the northern hemisphere.

The same was not true of the other continents. South America will spend almost the entire Oligocene separated from the rest of the world, developing a

Paw start
Since the Oligocene, the order Carnivora has evolved to include most large mammalian predators from bears and dogs to big cats and hyaenas.

unique range of creatures, including marsupials and armadillos. Africa, too, remains isolated until the closure of the Tethys Sea. Little is known of Oligocene Australia, but the slightly later Riversleigh rocks of Queensland suggest that its marsupials, such as the first kangaroos, are evolving rapidly.

In Antarctica, the continent responsible for much of the climate change in the Cenozoic, there is little evidence of life at all, possibly because by then it is already icing up. All in all, the Oligocene is far from being a quiet time. In many ways it is laying the foundations of the world we live in today.

Indricotheres

The most famous animals from Hsanda Gol are the giant indricotheres. These ancient members of the rhinoceros family grew to enormous sizes – the largest being found in the late Oligocene. They had long legs and necks for browsing on the tallest trees, like modern giraffes. The males were bigger than the females and had heavier, more dome-shaped skulls, which they may have used to butt each other while competing for females.

EVIDENCE: Many species of indricothere have been found across Eurasia, with the largest, from the Hsanda Gol, now called *Paraceratherium* (previously *Indricotherium* and *Baluchitherium*).

SIZE: The largest males were 4.5 metres (almost 15 feet) at the shoulder, weighing 15–20 tonnes (females around 11 tonnes).

DIET: Browsing on the upper branches of tall deciduous trees.

TIME: 30–25 million years ago.

Whether because he is concentrating so hard on the bone or because his senses are impaired by age, the old predator fails to notice the approach of a huge female indricothere. Standing almost 4.5 metres (almost 15 feet) at the shoulder and weighing over 11 tonnes, she makes surprisingly little noise as she walks towards the bluff. Indricotheres are distantly related to the rhinoceros, but have the long legs and neck of an animal that specializes in browsing on trees. This female's well-rounded silhouette against the moon reveals that she is pregnant, which explains why she is heading for the tall beech and elm of the river valley – she is looking for a safe place in which to give birth.

About 100 metres (330 feet) from the hyaenodon, her sensitive nose picks up the scent of the predator and she bellows out a warning. Caught completely by surprise, the old male leaps up and rounds on the newcomer, his hackles up and mouth wide open to display his teeth. The female continues her advance, waving her head from side to side and bellowing. This is a confrontation the hyaenodon is not going to win – the indricothere could smash his skull with one kick. Reluctantly he backs away, then with a yelp turns and runs off into the darkness. The indricothere stops and sniffs the air, issuing a few rumbling grunts. Bear dogs, disturbed by the confrontation, yap in the bushes round her and her large ears twitch as she tries to pick out any sounds of larger predators. After a moment she continues towards the taller trees further up the valley. Head down, her huge leathery shoulders push through the denser vegetation, cracking branches as she goes.

By the time she arrives in a clearing surrounded by elm, the moon is high. After inspecting the area she stops and shakes, dropping clumps of dried mud to the ground. She paces and snorts as waves of contractions grip her body. This carries on for about two hours before she spreads her back legs while emitting a series of low grunts. The birth itself is very

Mythical beasts

Cryptozoology means 'hidden wildlife' and involves the study of and search for animals whose existence is not confirmed by science. Perhaps the most famous examples are the Loch Ness Monster, Bigfoot and the Yeti. A lot of the giant mammals featured in this book died out comparatively recently – thousands rather than millions of years ago. Because of this many people have suggested that some are not extinct at all but are hidden in remote parts of the world waiting to be found – like the coelacanth, which was thought to have died out millions of years ago until a living specimen was caught off the coast of South Africa in 1938.

In Nandi, Kenya, there have for years been reports of a strange bear-like creature which supposedly lives in the forests in the centre of the country. Some cryptozoologists believe that the 'Nandi Bear', could in fact belong to a lost population of chalicotheres whose fossils indicate that they were found in the region within the last few hundred thousand years. Similarly, the strange snake-like body and sheer size of *Basilosaurus* have led some people to suggest that living examples of this ancient whale could be responsible for the many sightings of sea serpents. Other cases of missing animals include the mammoths, which some say still roam Siberia, and the Neanderthals, which are held responsible for Yeti sightings in the Himalayas.

One strange tale concerns the giant ground sloth *Megatherium*, which wandered the South American plains until only a few thousand years ago. The story goes that, in the early

Living relatives
A favourite source of cryptozoology stories is the existence of surviving ape-men – from Bigfoot to the Yeti (above). Every continent has its own 'hairy man' tales and even the evidence to prove it, such as this dubious Yeti scalp (right).

Nightmare beasts
Because of the sheer number of strange beast sightings, including giant cats and black dogs, some observers have turned to extinct mammals to explain the phenomenon.

1890s, an explorer reported that he had had a close encounter with an enormous, long-haired creature in Patagonia. His group had shot at the animal, but to no effect. Shortly afterwards, in 1895, an Argentinian rancher was said to have found a fresh-looking piece of *Megatherium* skin in a cave. The palaeontologist Florentino Ameghino got wind of these two stories and collected others from native Indians who also claimed that they knew of a large nocturnal beast which could not be killed with arrows. Ameghino went looking for what he assumed was a living *Megatherium* and recovered more pieces of hide and some dung, but no living creature. His hide samples were later carbon dated and found to be between 5000 and 10,000 years old.

quick. The female's waters break and a half-tonne baby indricothere receives a rude introduction to the world by falling 2 metres (6.5 feet) to the ground. It is a little male and as he tries to lift his head his new pink nose glistens in the moonlight. His mother stands to one side and watches him trying to struggle to his feet. Unfortunately, he is wallowing in gallons of birth fluid, which has turned the ground around him into a skating rink. He makes several attempts to get up, only to flop unceremoniously back down to the ground each time. His mother does not help   her baby's survival depends on his being able to stand on his own four feet from the start.

Suddenly the female picks up the scent of danger. Shadows are moving between the elms, and a pair of yellow eyes flashes as the unmistakable shape of a hyaenodon slinks into the clearing. It is not alone; there is a pair and at 3 metres (10 feet) long they are easily large enough to take a newborn indricothere. The mother positions herself over her infant and once again bellows in defiance. The predators work round opposite sides of the clearing, grinding their teeth in threat; their aim is to separate mother from baby. One hyaenodon moves forward and the mother charges, bucking her head. But her eyesight is not good and in the dim moonlight the hyaenodons have a distinct advantage.

Pick and choose: the teeth and muzzle of the indricothere mark it as a browsing animal, not a grazer. The molars are built to cope with a variety of softer vegetation, not hard grass, and the flexible lip helps it select choice greenery.

Facing the world
A little male indricothere looks out on an unfamiliar
world. Although he may appear vulnerable, his huge
mother, who towers over him, is quite capable of
seeing off any predators.

109

Amphicyonids (bear dogs)

These carnivores ranged from small, dog-like creatures to very large animals, which were more like modern grizzly bears. In fact they were neither bears nor dogs, but a group of their own related to both. Fossilized footprints show that they walked very much like modern bears, with their feet flat on the ground. They also lived in underground dens, and could probably dig out their prey if it outran them.

EVIDENCE: It was once thought that there were bear-dog fossils in the Hsanda Gol deposits, but these remains are now questioned. They were commonly found in Eurasia in the Oligocene, and it is likely that the dog-like types did live in Mongolia. They spread to North America, where well-preserved fossils, burrows and footprints have been found.

SIZE: The dog-like species were 30 centimetres (12 inches) at the shoulder.

DIET: They fed on small rodents and rabbits, which were common on the Mongolian plains at the time.

TIME: 40–9 million years ago.

Little terrors

Although the bear dogs on the plains are tiny compared to many of the creatures here, they are very efficient hunters of small mammals.

Unaware of the danger he is in, the newborn indricothere is still trying to rise to his feet. The second predator works her way closer, but bounds away as the protective giant returns. Again the baby is left alone and this time the first predator is swiftly on him. Catching one ear in his jaws he starts to drag him away. The little creature squeals in alarm, bringing his mother thundering back. The hyaenodon drops the baby and scrambles back among the trees. The mother stands over her prostrate infant, who

now has a badly torn ear. He is no longer lying in a pool of afterbirth and for the first time he manages to rise shakily to his feet.

Both mother and baby are exhausted, but there are still two hours to go until dawn and the hyaenodons are not about to give up. Again and again they sneak forward, only to be driven back by the giant female. The baby stands helplessly, unable to dodge the snapping jaws around him. His first night of life is going to be a long and dangerous one.

The world outside The sun rises quickly on the plains of Hsanda Gol and its rays reveal a rolling landscape covered in patchy forest and braided streams. Most rivers run on to the plains from the Elegan Mountains to the south and turn east before they reach the mighty wall of the Uskak Plateau. Between these two great boundaries lie thousands of square kilometres of open country. Along the river valleys walnut, elm, beech and pine cluster in dense stands. Elsewhere, lone oaks and pines dot the low hills. In between, shrubs cover the light dry soil, the most common plants being saltbush and ephedra. At this time of year, after the rains, the plains look quite lush, with annuals and flowers growing between the shrubs and new leaves on the trees. But this bounteous appearance belies the true nature of the place, which by mid dry season is almost a desert.

For now the mornings are moist and cold. At the bottom of the bluff a mother bear dog pokes her head out of her burrow to check that the coast is clear. Her breath leaves wisps of condensation in the air. She draws herself out fully and sits grooming in the entrance, her long thin tail curled round her. As her name suggests, she is ancestral to two very different groups of animals, bears and dogs, that will not evolve for millions of years.

From inside the burrow comes the sound of impatient youngsters. After a thorough wash the mother disappears down the hole and returns with two cubs. Together they set off towards a large watering hole to the east.

Entelodonts

These relatives of modern pigs were common in Mongolia. Many entelodont skulls have very severe wounds which were probably inflicted by other entelodonts during fights. The bony lumps all over their faces, like those of modern warthogs, were designed to protect delicate areas during these fights.

EVIDENCE: Partial skeletons are common in the Hsanda Gol fossil beds, but much better preserved and very similar fossils have been found in North America.

SIZE: Several species are known but the largest was about 2 metres (6 feet 6 inches) at the shoulder and weighed almost a tonne.

DIET: Their huge skulls were enormously powerful and designed to crush bones. Their thickly enamelled teeth are often broken, and show marks which suggest that they also chewed vines and exposed roots.

TIME: 45–25 million years ago.

As they wind their way through the saltbush they have to pick their way past a group of stocky hyracodons. These herbivores are very common on Hsanda Gol and distantly related to the mighty indricotheres, but they are only the size of large sheep.

At the watering hole, hyracodons line the shallows. They are nervous. At the other end a large mud-covered entelodont has also come down to drink. This fearsome-looking, aggressive creature is related to pigs and looks a bit like a gigantic cross between a boar and a warthog. Most of the animals on these plains are wary of entelodonts. The mother bear dog leads her cubs round the hyracodon to the opposite end.

The entelodont drops down on his knees to drink, the thick mud oozing up between his legs. Weighing close to a tonne, he is fast and powerful and will eat almost anything, though he is rarely seen to hunt. He specializes in scavenging carcasses, using his crushing back teeth to break open bones that many predators cannot cope with.

A low snort signals the arrival of the one creature who has nothing to fear from a grumpy entelodont – an indricothere. In the daylight it can be seen that her thick hide is a drab buff colour – with such poor eyesight and no need for camouflage, colours and patterns are not required. As she moves down to the edge of the pond a couple of eogrus ride on her back, crane-like birds that hunt for insects on her gigantic hide and in the vegetation she disturbs as she moves about. This is the mother who gave birth last night, but she drinks alone – there is no sign of her baby.

The entelodont ignores the new arrival and finds time for a bit of wallowing. But he is not left to enjoy his mud bath for long. Out of the trees comes a second entelodont. The newcomer marks a nearby tree as his rival struggles out of the mud to challenge him. Both animals open their mouths in an aggressive display, revealing huge gapes full of yellow tusks. The newcomer charges.

Here comes trouble
Entelodonts are powerful and short-tempered
animals. When they are not fighting with other beasts
over a carcass, they have violent confrontations
among themselves.

113

Piggy in the middle
Male entelodonts frequently
fight and their teeth, which are
designed to crush and pierce,
can inflict serious damage on
an opponent.

Jaws of death: an entelodont's gape is huge
and his teeth are built to do just about
anything – pierce, shear or crush. The
protrusions on the side of his face help
anchor muscles, but they may also protect
the more sensitive areas from attack.

All mouth

Entelodonts were vast and unsavoury beasts who bore a passing resemblance to modern-day warthogs, but are actually only distant relatives. When the first entelodont fossils were uncovered in America, nobody knew what to make of

It seems that entelodonts were important scavengers and used their powerful jaws to crack open bones and eat the marrow inside

them. They revealed a 1-tonne pig with massive jaws up to 1 metre (3 feet) long, far bigger than any modern pigs or their relatives. The role of these giant jaws was discovered by looking at the entelodonts' badly

chipped and cracked teeth, which were clearly designed for crushing. In America, palaeontologists found entelodont teeth marks on the fossilized bones of rhinos and brontotheres. It seems that entelodonts were important scavengers and used their powerful jaws to crack open bones and eat the marrow inside.

The teeth also show that as well as crushing bones entelodonts could eat practically anything. Recent work has found marks suggesting that they regularly scoffed vines, branches, tubers, hard fruits and nuts. They also didn't mind taking large bites out of each other. Some skulls tell stories of horrific violence with evidence of broken cheekbones, smashed eye-sockets and occasionally 2-centimetre (1-inch) deep bite marks across the muzzle. The teeth marks correspond to those of other entelodonts and it looks as if during these fights they would savage each other without mercy.

Fossil beauty
Entelodont skulls contain a wealth of information for scientists, but the most obvious revelation is that the animals must have been pretty ugly.

The whole water hole is thrown into confusion as the two massive beasts wheel round and round, thrashing and snapping at each other. Clouds of dust drift across the water and even the indricothere has to back away, her resident birds taking off in fright. Suddenly the entelodonts' mouths are locked and they stop moving. One has the snout of the other firmly clamped in his jaws but, at the same time, he has to endure a tusk driven straight into his lower jaw. It is a brief but agonizing trial of strength. Then the newcomer breaks away and flees, blood streaming from his nose. His vanquisher charges after him, tail held up rigid in triumph.

The water hole slowly returns to normal and the dust drifts off among the trees. The mother indricothere finishes her drink and heads back towards the bluff. Just short of the valley she stops and snorts. Sitting quite still among some young walnut trees is her baby, his skin pink and new in the morning sun. He climbs unsteadily to his feet and whinnies in response. One ear is caked with blood, but otherwise he appears to be intact. His mother must have done her job and held off the hyaenodons successfully.

The youngster stumbles out from the saplings, in urgent need of a meal. His mother towers over him, but she stands still and lets him search around for her teats. She has two tucked up between her hind legs, at least 2.5 metres (8 feet) off the ground. After a while the baby locates them and, with a bit of a stretch, manages to get a drink of milk.

The mother stands patiently, looking about for signs of danger. Finally she decides she has had enough and abruptly moves off. Her infant totters sideways and falls over. He gets up and scrambles after her at a trot, his one good ear waggling uncontrollably. When after a while his mother stops suddenly, he crumples into her back legs and sits down exhausted. She snorts aggressively and shakes her head. She has spotted another indricothere watching her from further down the line of the bluff. It is a male and unknown males are as big a danger to baby indricotheres as

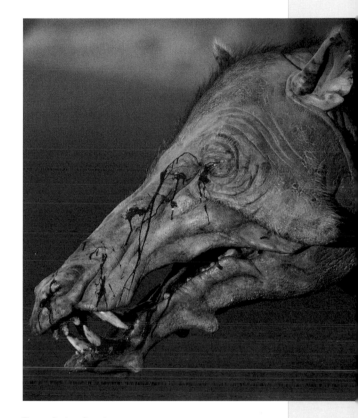

Down but not out
During fights entelodonts have been known to break cheekbones, smash eye-sockets and puncture sinuses. But only rarely are such wounds mortal.

117

hyaenodons. But this is a juvenile, probably only three years old, and rather than responding belligerently he starts to whinny. It is quite possible that he is the female's previous calf; if so, she would have been protecting him up until only a few weeks ago. Things have changed, though, now that she has a new calf. She makes to charge, but the juvenile is wise enough to retreat. The mother turns to check on her baby and then moves off to find food. The infant trots after her.

Milk bar
The baby indricothere will not be weaned for at least 12 months and during that time he will have to drink a lot of milk – for the mother, this is the downside of having such huge offspring.

First steps By midday the sun has pushed ground temperatures up to around 30 degrees. The indricothere calf is only nine hours old but he has already had to trot for 5 kilometres behind his mother, taking four tiny steps for each of her 2-metre- (6.5-feet-) long strides. The mother stops by a squat old oak tree and inspects the light green growth in its tallest branches. At full stretch she can pluck at leaves 6 metres (20 feet) off the ground. This feast is easily within her reach and with her long tongue and mobile top lip she begins stripping the branches bare. The calf feeds again and then stands blinking in the shade beneath her, looking out on his mother's Oligocene world.

This feast is easily within her reach and with her long tongue and mobile top lip she begins stripping the branches bare

Round the roots of the oak there is a low carpet of spiky-leaved plants that breaks up the saltbush. This is grass – a newcomer to the area but one that is destined to thrive in open country and, much later, with the help of grazing animals and humans, to dominate large tracts of the Earth. Small rabbits feed, oblivious to the giant next to them. Oligocene rabbits have not yet evolved the long ears and hopping back legs of their descendants, but they are developing a taste for grass.

Behind the indricothere, a number of white eogrus have landed and probe the ground for insects. Obviously emboldened by the fact that he is

Chalicotheres

By the end of the Oligocene, *Chalicotheres* had divided into two distinct groups. One lived in open areas and browsed like goats, the other was adapted to woodland and was more like a modern gorilla. These powerful animals shambled along carrying most of their weight on their short but strong hind legs. Curved claws meant that the *Chalicothere* could not put its front feet flat on the ground, and instead had to walk on its knuckles.

EVIDENCE: Fossils of a knuckle-walking *Chalicothere* called *Chalicotherium* from the late Oligocene have been found in Asia, but they are rare. Knuckle walkers are thought to have evolved in Asia much earlier, and so they are quite likely to have roamed in the wooded areas of Mongolia at this time.

SIZE: Height at rest: males 2.6 metres (8 feet 6 inches), females 1.8 metres (6 feet).

DIET: These *Chalicotheres* had no front teeth in the upper jaw, and even the back teeth show little wear, so they must have been fussy eaters, picking only the newest, freshest shoots and putting them into the back of their mouths like modern pandas.

TIME: 45–3.5 million years ago.

bigger than the creatures scampering round his mother and full of the sort of curiosity that all youngsters exhibit, the calf leaves the shade and heads for the eogrus. Ear flapping and head wagging, he runs back and forth, scaring the birds, which reluctantly rise, circle and return to the ground behind him.

After a while he starts on the rabbits. Small groups scatter in front of him but then rounding a saltbush he comes face to face with a nimravid. This beautiful cat-like predator, a member of the Carnivora order, has been stalking rabbits and is caught by surprise. It crouches and issues a high-pitched spitting sound. Despite only coming up to the calf's knees it is enough to send him scuttling back to his mother, where he rests under her reassuring belly.

Through the afternoon the mother indricothere divides her attention between three trees growing close together. The calf stays nearby, feeding when she will let him. The oaks are a short distance from a dense patch of beech and, as the day cools and the shadows lengthen, an adult chalicothere wanders out to feed on a patch of saplings.

Walking slowly on his knuckles, he takes his time to find the right place, then sits back with stomach bulging and uses his long arms to pluck at the small branches around him. His soft brown fur and dark eye patches give him a gentle look that disguises an extremely powerful animal. Closer inspection reveals long claws on the ends of his forearms which are quite capable of disembowelling a hyaenodon. In the forest, where they usually live, adult chalicotheres have few enemies.

The mother indricothere stops feeding and checks on her calf, who has discovered an abandoned bear-dog hole. She is becoming nervous. Evening is approaching and hyaenodons will soon be hunting again. She snorts and the infant once again takes up his position under her. Almost immediately she lets out a low warning call. She has spotted a hyaenodon stretching on

Green and pleasant land

An alien visiting this planet might be forgiven for thinking that grass was the dominant life form here. It covers vast areas of the globe and seems to have forced both grazing animals and farming humans into a dependent relationship designed to promote its spread. Grass is a comparative newcomer and yet, in the short time it has been around, it has had an enormous impact on life on Earth, making its evolution as important as the arrival of flowering plants in the time of dinosaurs.

Grass does not fossilize well and, although we can be reasonably certain that

Close crops
Once grass co-evolved with grazing herbivores, such as horses and deer, but more recently it has also developed a very close relationship with humans as a commercial crop.

no dinosaurs ever walked on grass, trying to pinpoint when this important group of plants evolved is difficult. The oldest definite grass fossils come from the late American Palaeocene (about 55 million years ago) and for the next 25 million years there are occasional fossil finds. It is clear that while grasses were present throughout much of the Cenozoic evolution of the mammals, they would have been rare. It is widely believed that the cooler and drier climate of the Oligocene gave the grasses their first break. As the tropical forests retreated towards the Equator, so the grasses would have been able to spread into the open patchwork of temperate forests left behind. Nobody can be exactly certain when the first proper grasslands appeared, although they were certainly in place by the middle Miocene.

Once fully evolved, grassland ecosystems were a major driving force in the evolution of mammals. To herbivores, the grasslands were a godsend, providing vast tracts of accessible, renewable food – renewable because no matter how much grass is grazed, it grows back from the root. However, it is a tough plant, impregnated with silica and difficult to digest. In order to utilize it, herbivorous mammals had to evolve new types of teeth

Beneath our feet
The human race has been described as grass's 'fairy godmother', granting it everything it could wish for to ensure its evolutionary success.

and specialized digestive systems. They also had to be able to travel great distances to find fresh areas of grass and to escape predators on the open plains. So, by the mid-Miocene, fast-moving grazing mammals had evolved on all the temperate continents.

There are some signs that grasslands may have appeared earlier in Oligocene Asia than they did elsewhere. In the Hsanda Gol, some of the fossil rodents and rabbits seem already to show adaptations that would have enabled them to cope with the tough leaves and stems of grass. If this is true, then it is possible that the Hsanda Gol floodplains could have been the earliest equivalent of our modern prairies, savannas and garden lawns.

a distant mound. As it yawns and scratches itself, a second appears beside it. The two greet and then descend the mound to set off into the saltbush. Already their brown and gold patterns are difficult to spot in the evening light among the scrub, but from her high position the indricothere can see that they are heading her way. She turns and cajoles her calf away. The chalicothere, meanwhile, has not spotted the predators. He is out of his forest sanctuary and unaware of the danger he is in.

Time passes and the hyaenodons have been working their way towards the chalicothere. This is a risky attack, but the herbivore weighs well over half a tonne and it would be a good kill. Keeping low, the predators split up and approach their quarry from different directions. When one is within 50 metres (160 feet) he suddenly stands up and runs straight towards his victim. The chalicothere honks in alarm and rises on his back legs to defend himself, his huge arms swiping at the on-coming hyaenodon. The attacker stops and bares his teeth. Before the chalicothere can land a blow, the second hyaenodon leaps on his back, sending him sprawling. Two vice-like jaws clamp on to the prostrate

Close to the knuckle: the chalicothere carries fearsome-looking claws for pulling down food and for defence. However, in order not to damage their long claws they have to walk on their knuckles, which means they can move only slowly.

Forewarned is forearmed
A mother chalicothere ushers her youngster away from a pair of resting hyaenodons. They are unlikely to attack such a powerful animal once they have lost the element of surprise.

Killing time

An old male chalicothere is ambushed by two hyaenodons. It is important that they lock on to his throat before he has a chance to beat them off with his powerful arms.

chalicothere, one grabbing an arm while the other searches out his neck. Although the victim flails with his free arm, he cannot dislodge the predators. Within seconds his fate is sealed.

Night is fast swamping the plains and as soon as the hyaenodons are sure their victim is dead they start to feed on it. They know they have to hurry because the sound of the kill and the smell of blood will attract other night-time hunters. A bear dog is the first of these to arrive and, although he is no match for the huge hyaenodons, he is faster than them and happy just to steal what he can. A couple of nimravids also appear and stalk round the carcass. The hyaenodons are tetchy and growl at the competition. One manages to chase the bear dog off into the darkness. But there is worse to come.

The hyaenodons have to hurry because the sound of the kill and the smell of blood will attract other night-time hunters

Out of the gloom trots an entelodont. The hyaenodons hunker down possessively over the body. Foolishly the huge pig comes closer. If there were other entelodonts with him they could well have seen off the predators, but since he is alone, the pair are in no mood to share. Suddenly they both turn on the pig. In the dust and chaos his fearsome snapping jaws keep them at bay, but it is a desperate defence and as soon as he gets the chance he turns and runs, pursued by the predators.

Fortunately for the entelodont, they soon abandon the chase and he stops among the saltbush and waits. More entelodont will arrive soon and then he will go back. Meanwhile, the hyaenodons return to the kill and have to clear a host of nimravids and bear dogs away. Soon they are crushing bones and tearing the body apart. A little way off, safe beneath the towering shadow of his mother, the indricothere calf picks up the smell of predators on the breeze and remembers.

On the run (OVERLEAF)
Outnumbered by hyaenodons, an entelodont is chased off a carcass. Frequently, however, the situation is reversed.

The long march A deep red sun sinks into the yellow haze that
hangs over the plains. The mountains to the south have been invisible for
weeks. It is midsummer and it is hard to believe that these plains could
possibly support so much life. Most of the trees have dropped their leaves
to save water and the skeletal oaks offer no shade. All the green herbs have
gone and a stiff breeze fills the air with a fine dust, painting all the scrub
brown. A herd of hyracodon stumble through the dust storms, heads down,
searching for vegetation. Here and there are patches of dark green where
evergreen trees cluster together. Sheltered from the wind next to one of
these stands the mother indricothere. She is covered in pale yellow dust and
dark tear stains run from her eyes down the side of her gigantic head. Below
her, sneezing and waggling his ears, is her infant. He is now six months old
and no longer fits so neatly under her belly. Under all the dust it is clear
that he has lost some of his original pink colour. Even his ear has healed.

   He tries to suckle but there is something wrong. His mother, her eyes
still shut against the dust, shifts her legs, pushing his head away. He tries
again and this time she is rougher, adding an aggressive snort. There are
many things that confuse and frighten the young indricothere, but his
mother has always been there to protect him. This is the first time she has
rejected him. He stumbles out into the dust clouds and whinnies in alarm.
He cannot appreciate that she has no milk for him, and that as her supply
has dwindled with the drought his suckling has become increasingly
painful for her. Over the last few days she has been able to find evergreen
food but no water – all her usual watering holes have dried up.

   Night comes and the mother starts to move in search of water. With
daytime temperatures so high, indricotheres travel at night to avoid
overheating. The female stops frequently, her sensitive nose sniffing the
dusty air for any hint of moisture. Her calf trots along behind. After an
hour or so the mother stops and this time issues a series of snorts and

Time to move on
During the drought season indricotheres mostly
move around at night to avoid overheating. They
will travel long distances in search of water.

Treasure hunters in the Gobi

Palaeontologists are not normally known for their recklessness, but Roy Chapman Andrews was the exception. He was an adventurer, reputedly the inspiration for Steven Spielberg's hero Indiana Jones, who discovered some of the most important known fossils, including the first extensive skeleton of the indricothere.

He also seems to have been blessed with a large amount of luck. In the 1920s Andrews, a former taxidermist who had joined the American Museum of Natural History in New York, became convinced that the hitherto unexplored and supposedly dangerous Gobi Desert of Mongolia contained a treasure store of fossils. In particular, he pushed the idea that the much sought-after evidence of the 'missing link' between humans and apes could be found there. Astonishingly, he managed to raise $250,000 to fund an expedition and, in April 1922, arrived in the Gobi with three cars, two trucks and 75 camels. Within days his party had hit the jackpot and were digging up dozens of giant dinosaur bones.

Andrews became something of a legend and the world gasped at his stories of having wrestled with bandits, survived sandstorms and traversed the roughest of

Indiana Jones
Roy Chapman Andrews was reputedly the inspiration for the famous film character and adventurer.

Creating a legend
Chapman Andrews' exploits on his expedition to Mongolia received worldwide publicity. He also collected superb fossil material.

terrain. He also stumbled across the Hsanda Gol formation, a set of rocks that has filled in a gap of several million years in the fossil record of Asian mammals. The expedition brought back the fossil remains of indricotheres, entelodonts and hyaenodons. One indricothere specimen had been preserved with its legs standing upright in the ground. Andrews said, 'Probably the beast had come to drink from

Whilst Andrews was undoubtedly a brilliant leader and courageous adventurer, some people paint a picture of him being in love more with his gun than with fossils

a pool of water covering treacherous quicksand. Suddenly it began to sink. The position of the legs showed that it had settled back upon it haunches, struggling desperately to free itself.'

Of late, however, Andrews' personal scientific contribution to these expeditions has been questioned. Although he was undoubtedly a brilliant leader and courageous adventurer, some people

paint a picture of him being in love more with his gun than with fossils. While the palaeontologists were hunting the desert floor for bones, Andrews was more likely to be out shooting for dinner. He never found any evidence of an ape/human missing link.

In 1930 political problems put an end to expeditions to the Gobi. Andrews eventually became director of the American Museum of Natural History, but he did not live long enough to see the reopening of these enormously rich fossil beds in the 1990s. They are once again changing our views of prehistory.

Bone bed
Although Andrews was best known for discovering dinosaur bones, his expeditions also found a lot of ancient mammal material, including this titanothere skull.

Died standing
Among his most famous finds were the four legs of a giant indricothere buried in an upright position, as if it had died after getting stuck in the mud.

bellows. Out of the darkness looms another female. Much older than the first, she has no calf with her. Female indricotheres are quite tolerant of one another and these two greet one another with a lot of sniffing. The older female then breaks away and moves off. The mother follows her, and is followed in turn by an increasingly distressed calf.

It is thought that indricotheres keep a very detailed map of their environment in their heads and that older animals in particular will remember thousands of square kilometres of the plains intimately. At times like this when water is short this information can save their lives. The old female is heading north for a watering hole she may have not used for years.

Again and again the little male tries to stop the long march so that he can suckle, but his mother rebuffs his efforts

Together the three indricotheres travel through the night, soon joined by two other gigantic females, both with calves. Again and again the little male tries to stop the long march so that he can suckle, but his mother rebuffs his efforts and he is forced to trail after them. By dawn they have moved over 80 kilometres (50 miles) and are close to the base of the Uskuk Plateau. The male calf is exhausted – he has not suckled for over a day.

A long bellow from the old female indicates that she has found what she is looking for. Over the lip of a rise they are presented with a huge expanse of dry lake bed but, in the centre, a spring-fed pond survives. Large blooms of algae cluster round the edge and thick clouds of insects dance over its surface. The indricotheres approach, driving a herd of nervous hyracodon aside.

At the water's edge they drink, ignored by the numerous crocodiles floating among the algae. Even the calves are too big for them to attack. The male staggers in the mud next to his mother and drinks. It will be a while before her milk returns so that he can suckle.

Parade of giants

Everyone is interested in records – the fastest animal, the tallest, the oldest and so on. But when it comes to extinct creatures there is one question that seems to fascinate more than any other – which was the biggest? It is incredibly difficult to estimate weights accurately from skeletons, but that does not stop people trying. The discoverers of the first indricotheres were quick to boast this was 'the biggest land mammal that ever lived'. Basing measurements on a few very large vertebrae and a toe bone, they claimed that the mass of the largest indricotheres was up to 'four and a half times as heavy as the heaviest recorded elephant [6.6 tonnes], and nearly twice the estimated weight of the heaviest mammoth'.

This 26-tonne creature would have been a very impressive animal, rivalling some of the largest dinosaurs. But those first reconstructions assumed that the indricothere had the same proportions as a modern rhino. In fact, it was rather like a stretched version, with longer legs and neck. Modern reconstructions put the indricothere's weight at roughly 11 tonnes, with the largest specimens (possibly the adult males) reaching 15–20 tonnes at the most. The largest of the Columbian mammoths are thought to have weighed

Biggest of them all
Even against fossils of other giant creatures, whales appear to be the largest animals to have evolved.

Mammoth find
Weathered out of a Norfolk cliff, this mammoth's thigh bone is the largest ever found, measuring 1.5 metres (5 feet) long.

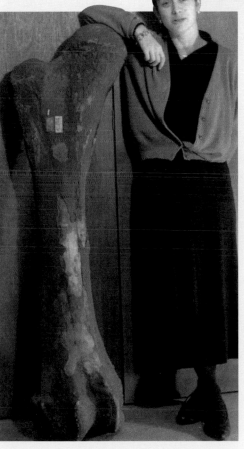

around 10 tonnes, so the indricotheres still hold the record, but not by very much.

Both indricothere and mammoth are dwarfed by other giants, however. In the water, the modern blue whale, at 150 tonnes, is still believed to be the largest animal that has ever lived. Marine creatures have a distinct advantage here. Firstly, the water supports their weight, so they do not have the structural problem of developing legs strong enough to carry a vast body. Also, because huge land animals have such a large volume of heat-generating body compared with their surface area they have a problem getting rid of heat. If you are floating in cold water, this is not an issue. These advantages, though, do not explain how the other group of giant animals, the sauropod dinosaurs, grew to be so huge, with maximums of around 70 tonnes. Many believe the key to this mystery lies in the sauropods' unique metabolism.

Different worlds

For the indricotheres flooded rivers are usually just an inconvenience, but for bear dogs they can be lethal, burying whole families in their burrows.

What's in a name? Bear dogs are so called because they are ancestral to both bears and dogs and exhibit a mixture of the characteristics of both animals. This particular Mongolian species is a little more dog than bear.

Life and death The wet season arrives with a few large raindrops falling out of a darkening sky and exploding on the dusty ground. Soon rain is drifting in great sheets across the plains, puddles become temporary lakes, rivulets form into rivers and streams into raging torrents. Every few days new storms sweep across and soon the earth is sodden. Waterways crisscross the plains and many animals seek refuge on raised ground.

Across one of these newly formed rivers the mother indricothere wades, followed by her struggling calf. Time and again the current lifts him off his feet and his head dips under, but he is a strong swimmer. Eventually the two reach the other side and the mother hauls herself up and over the high bank. Unfortunately this small obstacle for an adult presents the baby with a major challenge. The bank is wet and slippery. The infant tries to scrabble up, only to find himself very gently sliding back down. The harder he tries, the more slippery the slope becomes.

> The mother indricothere wades, followed by her struggling calf. Time and again the current lifts him off his feet and his head dips under, but he is a strong swimmer

While his mother waits patiently in the rain he throws himself at the bank, finally getting one foot and his head over the lip. It is not elegant, but he manages to drag himself to the top, stand up and shake off some of the mud.

Water levels are still rising fast and further down the bank the river is just below a bear-dog burrow. The mother bear dog looks out over a muddy torrent. She must have been asleep when the waters rose because she has left it too late to leave. Behind her two cubs jump and nip at her long tail. Before she can persuade them up to the entrance to swim for it, water starts to pour in and the tunnel begins to collapse. The family are forced deeper into the burrow, where they are quickly overwhelmed.

It is a small tragedy repeated across the plains, but altogether the rains are a life-giving force. Within weeks green shoots reappear everywhere and carpets of flowers spread between the saltbush. It is a good time for the animals here. A lot of the herbivores have their young now, which means there is a bounty for the predators. The indricothere calf is gradually gaining in confidence, happy to explore the environment further from his mother. He also spends a lot of time browsing – practising rolling his soft upper lip round branches and copying the food his mother eats, when he can reach it. Each day he grows larger and stronger and the threat from predators lessens. However, it will be some time before he can resist a hyaenodon attack.

A tall, dark stranger Months pass. The dry season comes and goes and the bond between mother and son remains strong even though he is weaned at just over a year old. With the new wet season the mother indricothere once again comes into oestrus. Initially this makes little difference to the calf, but life for his mother is about to become more hectic. The eogrus that sit lazily on her back will not be there for long.

The pheromones that the female leaves behind in her dung piles act like a beacon to male indricotheres. Soon the first suitor appears – an immature male. He sniffs the dung, snorts and smells the air. His upper lip curls up in a 'flehmen' reaction to the female's scent. He trots over to her, bucking his head and curling his upper lip to show a row of yellow teeth.

The female, however, is clearly not impressed. Female indricotheres are very careful about their choice of mate – most hold out for the largest and strongest males. This female wheels round and bucks at the male, who slows up and starts to circle. When she decides to leave, he follows after her, sniffing at her rump. She kicks out.

During all this the calf scampers along beside his mother, distressed and confused by what is going on. This is a dangerous time for the infant,

136

not only because he risks being accidentally hit by one of the adults, but also because excited males have been known to kill youngsters deliberately.

This particular ordeal does not last long because another much larger male appears. It is his territory and he has been tracking the female for some time. He is a huge animal, a lord of the plains, and at 15 tonnes nearly three times bigger than a bull African elephant. He bellows his intent. Then ominously yet another male appears, darker and older than the second suitor but just as large. The female must be on the edge of two territories. The youngest male backs away – clearly things are out of his league.

The second male approaches the female. Her calf hides behind her. The darker male intercepts his rival and the two stop to size each other up. With much snorting and kicking of dust they move closer together until they are standing side by side. Then the darker male swings his neck and, with a grunt, brings the top of his head crashing into the flanks of his opponent. Even though he has just received the sort of blow that could kill an entelodont, the other male stands his ground and then returns the favour. Male indricotheres' skulls are specially thickened on top in order to cope with this kind of challenge. Sometimes males carry on butting each other for hours. The female and her still-agitated calf move out of the combat zone towards a nearby oak where she starts feeding.

The fighting continues into the afternoon, when the darker male eventually manages to turn his opponent and chase him from the field of conflict. He returns, snorting in triumph, and starts to chase the female. Again she runs away but he is more insistent than his younger rival. In the chaos the calf is kicked to one side and winded. Before long the female stops and lets the bull indricothere mount her. While they are coupling the calf risks returning to his mother and tries to stand next to her. This is probably the most dangerous thing he has ever done, but fortunately the huge male ignores him.

Hard nuts
When two male indricotheres fight the forces involved are enormous. Because they use their heads to hit each other they have developed thickened skulls for protection.

Mating is short – the female can support the male's great weight for only a limited period. After a couple of minutes she moves and he dismounts. The calf continues to protest loudly and now the male turns his attention towards the youngster. The giant is in no mood to indulge him and he bellows in irritation.

Fortunately, at this point another male indricothere, attracted by the smell of the female, appears in the clearing. The instant the resident male spots him his priorities change. He will not tolerate any other male approaching the female, even after they have mated, so he turns his attention away from the calf and heads towards the interloper. Mother and baby rejoin and for a short time stand watching the new fight that has developed between the two males. Gradually the calf's calling dies away and then, perhaps realizing the danger her charge is in, the mother turns and hurries away.

Alone at last Two years pass and the mother and calf survive a particularly long drought, but despite the extreme conditions her pregnancy progresses well. The young male is now three years old and stands over 2 metres (6.5 feet) at the shoulder. He spends less time next to his mother, just occasionally exchanging nuzzling nose greetings. However, this cosy relationship is about to be shattered.

The wet season has spread another year's flush of green across the landscape and the plains are once again alive with the calls of mothers and babies. The indricotheres are feeding on a dense stand of beech and the calf moves round to pluck at the branches under his mother. Irritated by his presence, she swings her head, knocking him out the way. He retreats, confused. He watches his mother for a bit, then attempts to join her again. This time she is even more aggressive. She charges him and he is forced to flee. Several times he tries to come back but each time she repels him.

Dangerous position
During mating the calf continues to try to stay by his mother. In this situation males care little for youngsters and frequently either accidentally or even deliberately injure them.

Death of an ocean

While it lasts
Few summer visitors to the Mediterranean are aware that the sea as we know it is doomed because of the northward movement of Africa.

At the very end of the Oligocene, about 23 million years ago, as the indricotheres were roaming the plains of Asia, the movement of the continents finally destroyed an ancient and once prosperous ocean – the Tethys. From before the earliest times of the dinosaurs, over 220 million years ago, the Tethys had divided the giant southern continent of Gondwana from its northern counterpart Laurasia. As these landmasses split, twisted and manoeuvred their way across the surface of the Earth, an open ocean became trapped between Africa to the south and Europe and Asia to the north. By the start of the age of mammals (65 million years ago) all that was left was a long narrow arm of water running roughly from west to east and linking the newly formed Atlantic to the

the Oligocene, the continents collided in what is now Iran. But the death of the Tethys was not immediate. At first it was reduced to a series of thin, discontinuous seas referred to as the Paratethys Sea. Eventually any link between the Indian and Atlantic Oceans was lost and was not re-established until the opening of the Suez Canal in 1869. The disappearance of the sea from this region led to a much drier climate, with the rainforests retreating eastwards to the Malaysian Peninsula.

Today, all that remains of the ancient Tethys is the Mediterranean Sea, which was once its most western arm. This too is doomed and will eventually be squeezed out of existence by Africa's relentless push northwards. Not that the holiday resorts there have any immediate worries.

Any link between the Indian and Atlantic Oceans was lost and was not re-established until the building of the Suez Canal in 1869

older Indian Ocean. Despite their greatly reduced size, however, these waters still helped to support rainforest in what are now some of the driest places on Earth.

As the centuries passed, Africa and Arabia continued to push further north towards Eurasia and finally, at the end of

Here today
Tell-tale gypsum deposits, such as these in Israel, have been left by the Mediterranean completely evaporating, then refilling from the Atlantic.

All this signals that her time is near. The calf does not know it but his mother can be only a few days away from birth. Instinctively, she drives her older offspring away, because she cannot protect more than one youngster and the newborn will be vulnerable to a jealous sibling. Sometimes mothers tolerate the continued presence of another female but this calf is a male. As her mind turns its allegiance towards her unborn calf, the three-year-old becomes just another male and, as such, a threat. Bewildered, he watches his mother from afar, as another young male did three years before.

As night approaches the calf finds himself alone for the first time in his life. There are hardly any predators large enough to threaten him, but it won't be long before he is discovered by a hyaenodon. After watching his mother for a time he turns and disappears into the gloom.

Soon he catches the faintest whiff of a smell he has recognized since infancy, something that from the first hour of his birth he has associated with danger – hyaenodon. He turns and twists his large ears to try and detect where the threat is coming from. At the same time he squints into the darkness. There is quiet.

She drives her older offspring away, because she cannot protect more than one youngster and the newborn will be vulnerable to a jealous sibling

Then he hears it – a female hyaenodon stalking towards him through a stand of ephedra. He charges just as he has seen his mother do a thousand times. He carries nothing of her weight or experience, but he is in luck. Not only has he sensed correctly where the predator was, but there is only one, rather than a pair. The hyaenodon is forced to turn and run. Having lost the element of surprise, she abandons her hunt. The calf stops chasing and snorts after her. A white eogrus lands on his back. Now he really is standing on his own four feet.

4 The Prey's Revenge

Our world 3.2 million years ago

It is the mid-Pliocene and many pieces of the jigsaw are finally coming together to create a world that would be familiar to our modern eyes. Africa, Europe and Asia are all fused and the Americas will soon join. The trend towards a colder, drier climate continues and grasses enjoy an explosive success. There are still tropical forests at the Equator, but a third of the Earth's surface is now covered in some form of open grassland and here types of elephants, horses and antelope share the grazing just as they do today. Africa is the largest landmass to straddle the Equator and provides a retreat for many creatures escaping the advancing grasslands. One group of mammals that are forced in the mid-Pliocene to adapt to more open environments are the tree-dwelling primates. First the heavier, tailless apes evolve, and then a species with a more upright stance that allows it to move quickly between trees and over open ground in the search for food. This is the australopithecine and it will eventually give rise to one of the most bizarre creatures the world has ever seen – ourselves.

Dawn man (PREVIOUS PAGES) In the early dawn some australopithecines set off in search of food. These are the only group of primates that walk upright.

Death in the family It is a hot, still day and while most animals are resting in the shade a large porcupine is out in search of water. As he approaches an ancient acacia stand he stops to scratch at some of the many parasites that plague him. His long spines may save him from ending up on a lion's menu, but they also prevent him from grooming properly and make him a martyr to ticks and fleas. He shakes and carries on through the open ground beneath the trees. Ahead he can smell and hear running water. The acacia are crowded round a crystal-clear stream that tumbles over some large yellow rocks before spreading out and meandering among the parched boughs.

As the porcupine nears the banks he smells something else. Just upstream from him sit a group of australopithecines. These are large apes, but the porcupine knows he can resist their attention. What stops him drinking is the smell of death.

Lying half in and half out of the stream, with the cool water lapping round her lifeless features, is an old female australopithecine. There are no signs of violence – indeed, the poor condition of the animal suggests that she died of a prolonged illness, such as malaria. The other members of her group sit very quietly. A large male shuffles closer and leans over to sniff her. Satisfied that she is dead, he turns and wanders off into the forest to resume feeding. One by one the others follow him; they are all unusually quiet.

Finally, only one is left – a four-year-old male, who for the sake of identification is called Blue. His dark eyes are fixed on the corpse and he lets out a long, whimpering sound. It is his mother in the river and, although these australopithecines form very sociable groups, without his mother to teach and protect him, his future looks bleak. He would probably have stayed by her for hours had not the sight of a large porcupine washing upstream scared him and sent him stumbling off after the rest of the group.

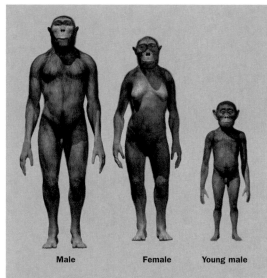

Male   **Female**   **Young male**

Australopithecus

Many species of these bipedal apes lived in southern and eastern Africa between about 4.5 and 1.5 million years ago. The animal in this chapter is *Australopithecus afarensis*, one of the older and more lightly built species.

EVIDENCE: *Australopithecus afarensis* is known from fossils found in Ethiopia (Hadar, Aramis), Tanzania (Laetoli) and Kenya (Omo, Lake Turkana, Koobi Fora, Lothagam). This species includes the famous fossil named 'Lucy', found at Hadar.

SIZE: Males 1.5 metres (5 feet) tall, females 1–1.2 metres (3 feet 3 inches–4 feet).

DIET: Varied, including fruit, tubers, nuts and probably some meat.

TIME: 3.9–3 million years ago.

Abandoned young
Blue is only four years old when his mother dies; without her his chances of survival are slim.

Land of our fathers

Peak districts
Many of today's major mountain ranges, such as the Himalayas, were established in the Miocene.

Although a map of the globe in the later Miocene and Pliocene epochs would have looked much as it does today, this period marked the start of the so-called Alpine Mountain Building phase. This saw the creation of the Alps, Himalayas, Andes and Rockies as well the start of the East African and Red Sea Rift Valleys. In addition to raising natural barriers to wildlife, these new mountains may have increased the average height of the continents enough to

disrupt the atmospheric air flow, shifting global rain patterns. Just as it does today, the Earth's rotation drove the weather from a predominantly westerly direction, giving the western sides of the continents more rainfall than the east. It was therefore largely on the eastern sides that the drier, more open grasslands were found.

By the start of the Pliocene most of the world's animals had evolved into basic body shapes that are recognizable in today's fauna. Pliocene deer, cows, cats, pigs, dogs, horses, elephants, rodents and rabbits looked little different from their modern equivalents. This is perhaps because the evolution of extensive grasslands during the Miocene provided a series of stable and relatively food-rich ecosystems, slowing the pace of adaptive evolution. This was particularly good for the hoofed animals, which were quick to develop grinding teeth and ruminating stomachs to exploit an all-grass diet.

By the mid-Pliocene the world had divided itself up into neat climatic regions ranging from the freezing ice caps through the wet temperate zones to the warmer tropics. Most parts of the world were still equably warm, with the extremes of climate, such as the tundra, very much confined to the northern and southern polar areas.

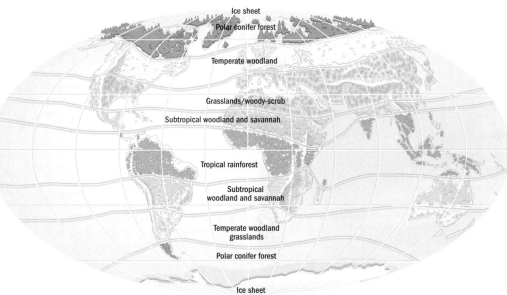

Open country
During the long Miocene the continents began to take on their modern configuration. Africa's northward march finally split the Tethys sea creating the Mediterranean. However, on the other side of the globe South America was still isolated. There

was now ice at both poles, which helped to establish new vegetation belts from coniferous high-latitude forests to rainforest round the equator. Significantly, the ice had dried the climate, resulting in vast grasslands, especially in temperate regions.

Joined continents and a less severe climate allowed many animals to migrate far and wide across the globe. What are now considered to be tropical animals, such as hyaenas, lions and camels, were found in North America, Europe, Africa and Asia. In London's Trafalgar Square hippos and elephants would have basked around a warm swampy river. The climate may not have been as hot as during previous Cenozoic epochs, but it certainly wasn't cold either.

The oceans, too, were being invigorated by the increased circulation of water coming from the north and south polar regions. Plankton bloomed on the nutrients provided by these ocean currents. In turn, fish would feed on the plankton and other animals such as sharks on the fish. The whales were thriving and evolved smaller species like the dolphins.

All in all the Pliocene was a time of relative success before the onset of the turbulent ice ages. Animals did well in this grassy open world and in Africa our first ancestors came down from the trees to exploit the plains. Life was almost literally making hay while the sun shone, but the darker days of the Pleistocene were looming, when the world would be in for a cold shock.

Whale of a time
Whales continued to do well in the oceans, evolving giant plankton-feeding forms as well as the smaller, toothed dolphins.

Sunnier times
Evidence of how different the climate was before the ice ages began comes from the hippo bones which scientists have found beneath Trafalgar Square, in London – and these bones did not come from the zoo.

Home, sweet home This area of eastern Africa is a haven for wildlife. It is geologically very active, but the climate supports an abundance of animals and plants. Between the volcanic peaks is a mosaic of grassland savanna, open woodland and dense tropical forest. This variety of habitats is reflected in the range of animals that shelter here. Plains creatures such as antelopes, elephants and horses live close to forest dwellers like primates, bats and pigs.

One animal that has developed a unique ability to move easily between these two habitats is the australopithecine ape. Equally at home clambering among the trees in search of fruit or digging in more open ground for roots, groups of australopithecines are dotted all over this area. The reason for their success lies in their adaptability. They are extraordinarily intelligent animals, constantly adjusting to situations and exhibiting highly sophisticated social behaviour.

The 'acacia group' of australopithecines formed about 15 years ago when a larger community to the north split and three males and four females moved south out of the dense antrocaryon forest into the more open mahogany and acacia woods. With the death of the old female only one adult from the original seven is left – Greybeard – and he has been the dominant male for the last seven years. With him there are now three other females – Babble, Berry and Blackeye – and a large young male, Bruiser. Babble and Berry both have young, and then there is the newly orphaned Blue.

Relationships within the group are highly political. Although Greybeard is still very much in charge, he knows Bruiser is waiting to challenge him.

> Equally at home clambering among the trees in search of fruit or digging in more open ground for roots, groups of australopithecines are dotted all over this area

Although australopithecines have developed an upright gait, their feet and toes are still well adapted for the trees – helping them cope with both environments.

Look out
Berry stares out at her spectacular African home in the Great Rift Valley, unaware of the forces that have created it.

Walk the walk

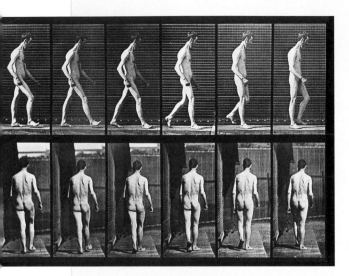

Walk tall

Although there are many features that separate humans from apes – such as brain size and lack of hair – the defining characteristic that sent us off on a different evolutionary path seems to have been an upright stance.

Jungle man

Research shows that orangutans developed their own method of upright walking for moving along branches. Human gait could have evolved from this sort of activity.

As soon as palaeontologists saw the upper leg bone of the famous australopithecine fossil, Lucy, (see pages 176–7), they knew that this was a creature that walked on its hind legs. However, although everyone agreed that Lucy could walk on two legs, there was by no means a consensus on what she looked like when she did. When chimpanzees walk upright, they don't have the flowing stride of humans. Instead, they adopt an almost crouching position; their knees slightly bent and their bodies leaning forwards at the hip. Walking as we do was seen as a vitally important stage in human evolution – somehow defining the starting point for being human.

However, recent work by Robin Crompton and his team in Liverpool has somewhat refined this view. By carefully studying the ways in which different apes walk, and by building a computer model of Lucy's skeleton, they have shown that Lucy simply could not have walked like a chimpanzee, with a bent knee and hip.

Although she could have moved like a modern human, there was in fact a third way of walking on two legs that would have been even more efficient for an animal with her proportions – the method used by a modern orangutan. They walk on two legs along branches, using their long arms to hold on to other vegetation for balance, allowing them to reach for fruit at the top of trees. Robin Crompton's group have found that an orangutan's gait is much more similar to a human's than it is to a chimp's, and it suits Lucy's skeletal proportions very well.

This research suggests that maybe walking on two legs was actually an adaptation to living in a jungle, and that when our ancestors first made strides across the plains they were only continuing a 'walk' they had developed in the trees. As for defining what is human, that would mean that orangutans now become honorary humans.

It is important for him to keep the support of the adult females and the loss of Blue's mother, one of his most loyal supporters, has upset the balance. In the days after her death Bruiser shows signs of aggression and this creates tension within the group.

One afternoon the apes move to very edge of the woodland to feed on jackal berry bushes. They all arrive walking on two legs – another unique feature of these primates. It would appear that, since they spend so much time in the open, this posture allows them to move about more efficiently. It also makes them faster than their knuckle-walking ape relatives and, since they are more vulnerable to large predators on the ground, this is important.

As is now usual, Blue arrives some time after the rest and has difficulty reaching the berries. Until a couple of weeks ago, his mother would have been there to help him feed but now he is on his own and the other australopithecines ignore him. When he eventually finds some food Berry's baby takes it from him, but he does not dare resist, knowing that Berry would attack him if he does. Another loss Blue must now overcome is the absence of the intense social bonding he experienced with his mother. While she was alive, he would spend large parts of the day sitting next to her while she groomed him. None of the other females in the group is able or willing to adopt a dependant, so he is going to have to learn to grow up very quickly.

Nearby, on the open savanna, a herd of magnificent deinotherium are destroying a lone acacia. These ancient cousins of the elephants use their downward-facing tusks to strip the bark off the tree and, as if that wasn't enough, after they have eaten all the bark they can reach, they use their weight and short muscular trunks to push the whole tree over and strip the upper branches. Without the activities of deinotherium herds, the woodlands would be far more extensive.

Deinotherium
The deinotheres were gigantic but little-known cousins of the elephants which flourished at the time of the australopithecines. Tusks in the elephant family have continually varied in shape and size as they have been used for different purposes. Wear marks on the downward-curved tusks of *Deinotherium* suggest that they were probably used for stripping bark.
EVIDENCE: *Deinotherium* remains – particularly their tusks and teeth – occur at all the major excavation sites in East Africa where hominids have been found, including Hadar, Laetoli, Olduvai Gorge and Lake Turkana.
SIZE: Males 4 metres (13 feet) at the shoulder, females 3.5 metres (11 feet 6 inches).
DIET: Browsed vegetation and stripped bark.
TIME: 20–1.5 million years ago.

The apes ignore the elephants while they cram their mouths with soft berries. Unusually, Bruiser does not join in the feeding. For a time he watches, then he breaks off a branch and starts dragging it round, shrieking and chattering. It is a direct challenge to Greybeard. The older male ignores the show of aggression, but the females around him are getting nervous. Babble and her youngster have to run out of the way as Bruiser works his way closer to Greybeard. Just as it looks as though things are going to get out of hand, Blackeye starts hooting with alarm. The deinotherium have finished destroying the acacia and, attracted by the commotion, are heading towards the group. Greybeard stands up, grabs a

Deinotherium tusks, unlike those of many other types of elephants, grow from their lower jaws like fangs. Together with a short strong trunk, this helps them strip bark off trees.

African giant
The male deinotherium stands well over 4 metres (13 feet) tall, weighing around 6 tonnes. At this size he has no natural predators, even in Pliocene Africa.

Long in the tooth

Perhaps the most striking aspects of a living elephant's anatomy are its tusks. Although they are an ancient feature of this group, over the years elephants have experimented with an extraordinary variety of shapes.

A tusk is simply a tooth (normally an incisor) which keeps growing throughout the animal's life, eventually forming a thick and elongated tube of ivory. A modern African bull elephant's tusks may be as long as 3 metres (10 feet) and weigh up to 120 kilograms (265 lb). But this is small compared with the tusks of some of their fossil ancestors. The most inconvenient tusks belonged to the extinct *Anancus* – at 4 metres (13 feet), these were as long as its body and stuck out straight in front of it. They were probably used to search for food amongst forest leaf litter. The award for the largest of all time must go to the European mammoth, whose spiralling tusks could reach a staggering 5.5 metres (18 feet) in length.

Although we think of elephant tusks as emanating from the upper jaw, this has not always been the case. Two different groups of elephants abandoned their upper-jaw tusks in favour of lower-jaw ones. The gomphotheres evolved huge spade-like lower teeth that protruded well beyond the

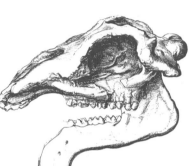

Mystery mouth
The bizarre shape of the *Deinotherium*'s tusks has puzzled scientists since their first discovery.

Unnatural selection
Seven tonnes of confiscated ivory burn in 1991. In recent decades man has turned the tusk into a selective disadvantage.

Frozen treasure
Ironically, with a ban on trade in elephant ivory, the trade in mammoth ivory pulled out of the permafrost has actually grown.

jaw line, making them look a little like a fork-lift truck! These animals lived near water and it is thought that the flattened teeth were used to drag plants from riverbeds. Just as bizarre were the deinotheres, which had short and sharp lower tusks that curved downwards below their jaw, like fangs. Nobody is really sure why the deinotheres should have developed this unique adaptation.

In the modern world, tusks became a liability. Ivory is a much valued commodity and during the 1970s so many wild elephants were killed for their tusks that they faced extinction. A worldwide ban on ivory trading has changed this situation, but has had an unforeseen effect on another elephant species. There is currently a thriving trade in ivory from the millions of fossilized mammoth tusks that can still be found in Siberia.

Out of Africa

Race relations
In evolutionary terms the differences between the human races are insignificant, but the social importance of race has ensured that origins have attracted much debate.

First travellers
Homo erectus was the first hominid to escape the mother continent and spread across the world. These fossils belong to Peking Man, found in Asia.

It was Charles Darwin who first suggested that humans might have originated in Africa and dispersed from there all over the globe. Since the African apes were clearly our closest living relatives, and the australopithecines, our ancestors, were found only in Africa, this seemed the most likely place for us to have evolved. But for some time there has been controversy about exactly when we decided to leave our mother continent and, depending on whom you believe, it fundamentally affects our concepts of race.

Fossils show that about 1.5 million years ago, one of our ancestors, *Homo erectus,* migrated out of Africa and lived in many areas around the world. Some scientists, in what is called the multiregional hypothesis, then suggested that *Homo erectus* evolved separately into *Homo sapiens* in Asia, Australasia, Europe, etc. The controversial consequence of this theory is that present human races – Chinese, Caucasian, African, etc. – are much more separate than were first thought.

However, more recently, a second theory has challenged this, suggesting that *Homo sapiens* evolved in Africa only about 150,000 years ago and was responsible for a second wave of migration, eventually replacing all the

Homo erectus. This was called the 'Out of Africa' hypothesis and it suggested that all the races were in fact much more closely related than supporters of the multiregional hypothesis believed.

Fossil evidence could not resolve this without a lot more samples, but initially support for the second theory came from a surprising quarter – genetics. Geneticists analyzed DNA sequences from the Y chromosome (which is passed from father to son) and from the mitochondria (which are passed from mother to daughter). This suggested that all the people alive today came from a group which lived in Africa and, more significantly, only about 150,000 years ago. These results have since been questioned. The controversy and sensitivity surrounding the physical origin of races ensures that research in this area attracts much debate.

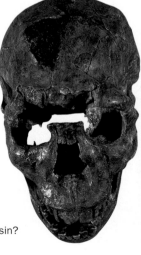

That is the question...
When studying new fossil humans, one question is always asked: Is this a direct ancestor or a distant cousin?

dead branch and starts thumping the ground with it; then he heads off into the denser woodland. The females follow him and Bruiser drops his branch and does the same. Just before a large tusker arrives at the jackal berry bushes, Blue grabs some dropped berries and lopes off after Bruiser.

Two days later the group are feeding near a large cascading waterfall. Babble is showing her daughter the peculiar delights of acacia sap, which australopithecines use like chewing gum. Blue sits close by, but is not included in the lesson. He is not well and has a bad case of diarrhoea. Again, if he had the care of a mother she would show him that eating myrtle leaves is good for this condition. As it is, he will just have to survive without. It is desperately important that he starts to form his own social links within the group because, although they tolerate him, he needs to reinvent his role.

Suddenly Bruiser, who has been in the lower branches of a tree, comes crashing down towards Greybeard, shrieking and waving vegetation. Greybeard stands up and both males puff out their chests and start shoving one another. The whole group jabber and call at this outbreak of violence. Bruiser once again breaks off a branch and drags it around, but he is charged by Greybeard, who gives him a flying cuff across the head. While Bruiser recovers, Greybeard runs to the edge of the stream and starts throwing pebbles and rocks at his opponent. Bruiser is coming off worse and it is clear that Greybeard is not going to surrender his position without a fight.

As quickly as the violence started, it is over. In triumph Greybeard mates with Blackeye, but in a new development Babble goes over to groom Bruiser. The challenger is down but not defeated.

> Both males puff out their chests and start shoving one another. The whole group jabber and call at this outbreak of violence

155

Time to relocate A ripe fig tree has drawn the acacia group to the edge of the forest in the northern part of their territory. These primates spend 60 per cent of their waking time feeding. While Blackeye and Greybeard climb among the branches to pick fruit, the rest sit round the base, feeding on the fallen ones. Blue sits next to Babble, holding out his hand for food. Australopithecine mothers usually care for their young for up to five years, so at four Blue is struggling to be independent. But Babble has her own youngster to concentrate on and ignores Blue.

The tree is near a river that runs out of the forest and on to the savanna. There are giant otters here that can attack and kill young australopithecines. Today there don't seem to be any about, but instead a much bigger threat arrives. Six male australopithecines appear on the other bank, shrieking and throwing stones. Greybeard reacts quickly, standing up, baring his teeth and waving his arms. The australopithecines are a hunting party intent on displacing or even killing others of their kind. The acacia group must win this confrontation if they are to hold on to their territory. After a long series of challenges, Greybeard charges the other males, splashing across the shallow river and throwing stones. He is a large ape and four of the challengers quickly disappear back into the forest. But the other two stand their ground and Greybeard stops short of physical contact. Soon the four males reappear and all six charge Greybeard. He is instantly overwhelmed and receives blow after blow as he tries to retreat back across the river.

By now the acacia group are in turmoil – the females pick up their young and flee. Bruiser offers the defeated Greybeard no help as they run from their attackers. In all the chaos Blue is left far behind. He is lucky that none of the males find him, because they might well kill and eat him, but as the acacia group get further and further away his chances of survival are looking bleaker. He still hasn't learned to find food for himself and he would make a small snack for a leopard.

Territorial dispute
The acacia group are threatened by a much larger group from the north. These disputes are regular occurrences but, with numbers so low in the acacia group, their survival is threatened.

Last of the ancients
Chalicotheres used to be a
varied and widely distributed
group of animals, but now
ancylotherium is one of the
last of a dying group.

Many earlier species of chalicothere walked
on their knuckles so they could support
large claws, but ancylotherium has more
conventional hoof-like feet.

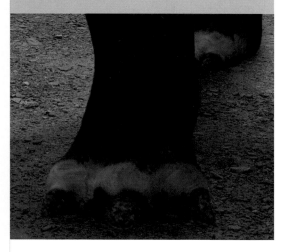

On the move With only two adult males the acacia group have little chance of holding on to their territory for long. Over the next few days there are further confrontations and finally the group is forced out of the woodland completely. The open ground where they now find themselves is dangerous for them. They are still primarily wood and forest creatures and need trees to live in and as sanctuary from attack. So Greybeard immediately heads for another patch of woodland. As he does so, the group string out in a line to cross an open volcanic ash field. Although their ultimate aim is to find new territory, their immediate problem is water. They all need to drink.

Surprisingly, jumping in the footsteps the group have left in the ash, Blue is following only about 100 metres (330 feet) behind. He must have caught up with the rest of the group as they moved round their territory to escape their attackers, and so he did not miss their exit from the woodland. Despite all his hardship, Blue is showing remarkable resilience and as he bounces along behind the others there is even a suggestion that he is playing.

Greybeard leads them all to a waterhole just the other side of the ash field. A herd of gentle ancylotherium are already drinking there and they ignore the arrival of the apes. Fully grown, these animals are over 2 metres (6.5 feet) tall and weigh around half a tonne, far too big to be threatened by apes. They are one of the last of a group of animals called the chalicotheres, some of whom were giant knuckle-walkers. Ancylotherium browse on low branches, a bit like goats, but are otherwise more conventional four-legged herbivores. The australopithecines gather next to the herd to drink while the two babies play at the water's edge. The group show different approaches to drinking – some lower their heads to the water, others cup their hands and drink from them, but Babble gathers leaves and uses them to soak up water like a sponge.

Ancylotherium
One of the last surviving chalicotheres, *Ancylotherium* was a cousin of the bizarre knuckle-walker featured in Chapter 3. It was built rather like a large goat, adapted to reach up and browse the vegetation studding the plains of Africa, just as its ancestors had done all across the plains of Europe, Asia and North America.
EVIDENCE: Sparse remains of *Ancylotherium* have been found at many of the most famous hominid fossil sites in East and South Africa, including Laetoli, Olduvai Gorge and Omo.
SIZE: 2 metres (6 feet 6 inches) at the shoulder.
DIET: Browsed vegetation.
TIME: 6.5–2 million years ago.

On their guard (OVERLEAF)
Waterholes are good feeding areas for australopithecines, but in the open there is a danger not only from predators, but also from aggressive herbivores like the deinotherium.

All musth go
Fired up by hormones, the male deinotherium can become dangerously aggressive and will attack even harmless creatures.

It is because she is doing this that she is the first to spot the approaching male deinotherium. His smell and the weeping temporal glands on the side of his head immediately indicate he is in musth – a state of frenzied excitement that means he is eager to mate – and a very dangerous animal to be near. The ancylotherium quickly scatter, but the australopithecines have to head for a group of trees on the other side of the lake for safety. They run, but Babble's youngster is still by the water and the deinotherium is approaching fast. The mother calls out, but the little ape is too frightened and confused to respond. As the rest of the group swiftly retreat to the trees, Babble remains on the ground, desperate to reach her baby, but too afraid of the unpredictable giant to return to the water's edge and collect him.

Her screeching is clearly disturbing the deinotherium and instead of drinking he heads for the trees where the group are. The baby is safe, but the rest of the australopithecines are now in trouble. Babble deftly swings into the trees as the deinotherium draws near. At first he just trumpets at them, shaking his head and displaying his saliva-covered tusks. But then he rams the nearest tree violently. Although these are massive trees and he will never topple one, it is still time for the group to move on. The forest is quite open, but they move easily through the branches and where boughs do not connect they drop down to run between trees. Only Babble doesn't follow Greybeard. She works her way sideways and then runs across and grabs her baby. As she flees into the woods the deinotherium is momentarily distracted, but he then goes back to pushing at the stout tree which is now empty of australopithecines.

Blue is late as usual, but on this occasion it allows him to witness the whole episode from a safe distance and take a drink. He watches the commotion while sitting next to a pile of deinotherium dung. Driven by hunger he sniffs it and then starts to eat it. This is not odd behaviour – he

Tree top trap
Deinotherium frequently use their size and power to push trees over so they can graze on their leaves. As a result the branches of even the tallest trees are not necessarily a safe place for the primates.

might even have learned it from his mother. The dung contains nutrients for the ape even though the deinotherium's digestive system can get no more out of it. But when Blue sees the group head off into the woods, he stops feeding and skirts round the lake after them.

Around dusk the group stop to build nests, something australopithecines do every night. In heavily forested areas the nests can be quite elaborate, but here in this woodland they are very simple. An ape's nest is his castle and no other ape, no matter where he appears in the pecking order, can disturb another's sleep. Blue still has much to learn about constructing nests, but before his mother died he had at least started to build his own, although it still involves a lot of trial and error.

An ape's nest is his castle and no other ape, no matter where he is in the pecking order, can disturb another's sleep

While he is pulling branches down around him to form a loose platform, his attention is drawn to Babble's baby, who is playing on a branch. He walks along the branch and sits close by, watching her. The youngster starts to play-fight with Blue, cuffing and wrestling with him. It is an important moment for the orphan, because it is the first time since the death of his mother that a member of the group has acknowledged him. Unfortunately he gets overexcited, the play becomes too rough and the youngster cries out. Babble is there in seconds, grabbing Blue and trying to bite him. The whole group is in uproar. Bruiser joins in the fight and luckily breaks it up before Babble can inflict real damage. Blue scampers over to his nest for sanctuary. Ironically, despite the violence of the confrontation, this was good for him. Both Babble's baby and Bruiser seem to acknowledge him as part of the group. This cannot happen too soon for Blue – he is looking very thin and is certainly not as large as he should be at his age.

Dream time
Every evening the group seek out trees to build
nests in. It would be too dangerous to spend the
night sleeping on open ground.

Dinofelis
One of the big sabre-toothed cats, with several species spread across North America, Europe and Asia as well as Africa. It was built rather like a modern jaguar, but with more powerful front legs, which meant that it probably ambushed its prey and used the front legs to hold it down firmly while it made a clean kill with its teeth.
EVIDENCE: *Dinofelis* is relatively rare, but its remains are found in conjunction with hominid fossil sites.
SIZE: 1 metre (3 feet) at the shoulder.
DIET: Antelope, baboons and australopithecines.
TIME: 5–1.4 million years ago.

Pastures new The days pass and although the acacia group do not move far they take another couple of weeks to settle in a new territory. About 50 kilometres (30 miles) south of their original home they find an area dominated by pod mahogany trees. These are ideal for making nests in and can also have tasty fruit. There are no other australopithecine groups around and so there is a fair chance that they will do well here. However, it is very close to the savanna and there is danger in this woodland that is not immediately apparent.

Late one afternoon Greybeard and the females find a cross berry bush. Its soft fruit is a favourite with the apes and they all drop down from the trees to strip it. Nearby are the burrows of a dwarf mongoose colony and while the group feed a hunting party returns. The mongooses rush around the australopithecines, greeting and rolling over each other, but ignoring the apes completely. These active little hunters know exactly what and what not to fear. Gradually they retreat down their burrow, but five or six remain above on look-out duty.

At this point Bruiser arrives, cradling an ostrich egg in his arms. Gently he hoots and rolls the egg on the ground, then scampers back and forth to attract attention. Greybeard conspicuously ignores him, but the others are curious. In particular, Babble wanders over to sniff the egg. After showing off for a while, Bruiser comes back to the egg, carrying a stone. He thumps at the shell several times and, having created a small hole, dips his finger inside to pull out the yolk. Babble and Berry abandon the fruit and join Bruiser for a taste of egg.

Greybeard is now getting angry. He picks up a stick and drags it around where Bruiser and the others are feeding. The mongooses shriek and disappear down their burrow, but this is not because of the fight between the two males. The warning is there, but the apes are too preoccupied to notice. Blackeye is sitting alone by the cross berry bush as a huge pale-

The expressive primate face is an essential tool of communication within the social structure of the group. The expression of terror here is an instant warning signal to others in the group if they have failed to notice the rather large predator nearby.

Moment of terror

Since the dinofelis can also climb trees, the australopithecines are only safe as long as they can deter the cat from following them into the high branches.

Cat's people
The extinct sabre-toothed *Dinofelis* was similar to modern leopards, although it was larger and would have had no problem killing australopithecines.

The original manhunter

While the sabre-toothed cat *Dinofelis* did not have the impressive canine teeth of some of its relatives, it may be that it represented our ancestors' worst nightmare. When the first australopithecine fossils were found in 1925, they were in caves alongside the remains of common prey animals that seemed to have met a violent death. In the light of modern hunter-gatherer societies, the bones' discoverer, Raymond Dart, announced our ancestors were 'killer apes'. Australopithecines seemed to have marked the first divergence from the other apes in more than just body – they were developing the human hunter's mind. By the 1970s, though, opinions started to change. One researcher, Charles Brain, reanalysed the mixture of hominid and other animal remains and found that it consisted of large numbers of australopithecines and baboons, along with the occasional remains of big cats. Then one startling piece of evidence came to light – the skull of an australopithecine child with distinct leopard toothmarks imprinted in it. Brain proposed that rather than being killer apes, the australopithecines had been the victims. He suggested that either the bones had been brought there by the big cats or that the apes had lived in the caves and the cats sneaked in and killed them while they slept.

Since so many of the bones belonged to primates, this looked like the work of a specialist feline manhunter. Leopard teeth fitted the damage on the child's skull, but some of the prey items in the caves were too large to have been killed by leopards. There was only one cat big enough to have committed the crimes – the sabre-toothed *Dinofelis*. Australopithecines would have been small prey for such a powerful cat, but perhaps it developed a taste for hominid flesh and simply picked off our vegetarian ancestors as easy meat.

Some of the prey items in the caves were too large to have been killed by leopards. There was only one cat big enough to have committed the crimes – the sabre-toothed *Dinofelis*

Bone crusher
The heavily-built skull of *Dinofelis* was easily strong enough to crush a hominid skull.

Teeth marks
Two perforations just visible in this australopithecines' skull exactly match the canines of a leopard.

coloured creature streaks across the ground towards her. She does not stand a chance.

The sabre-toothed cat, dinofelis, is an ambush predator with powerful front limbs and a crushing bite. Blackeye has no more than a moment to cry out before she is bowled over and pinned down. Attacking a large ancylotherium the dinofelis might have gone for the throat, but with the ape he just crushes her skull. It is all over even before the rest of the group have time to react. Then, with an almost simultaneous screech from four throats, they scramble for the nearest trees. Shrieking in alarm and terror they race about the branches, shaking leaves and staring at the sorry sight below. The dinofelis adjusts his grip on Blackeye so that he has her neck in his mouth. Then he half lifts her and starts to drag her away from her distraught companions.

Big cats are the main predators of australopithecines, especially smaller species such as leopards, which can climb into the trees in pursuit of their prey. Dinofelis usually attack larger prey, but if this particular one develops a taste for apes then the group is in trouble. The sabre-tooth drags Blackeye to a large mahogany tree that leans over a deep limestone sinkhole and then, using his incredibly strong forelegs and neck, manages to carry her up into the lower branches. Despite his size and power the dinofelis knows that the smell of the kill will attract competition, particularly from hyaenas. If he is outnumbered he can be chased off a kill before he has managed to eat his fill. In the tree he can eat the carcass in peace, or leave it and return to it later until the whole kill is finished or has fallen into the sinkhole.

> Big cats are the main predators of australopithecines, especially smaller species such as leopards, which can climb into the trees in pursuit of their prey

All change It is several days since the dinofelis attack and the group are sitting in some lower branches indulging in mutual grooming. Blue is grooming Greybeard, earnestly picking away at the hairs on the back of his neck. This is an enormous step forward for the youngster – it means he is beginning to establish himself and, although he is right at the bottom of the pecking order, he now stands a good chance of seeing adulthood. The death of Blackeye was a blow for all the group, but particularly for Greybeard. She was very loyal to him, and with her gone, his tenuous grip on power is slipping. Only a short distance away he is being watched by Bruiser and, what is more worrying, Bruiser is once again being groomed by Babble.

As if all this were not presenting Greybeard with a difficult enough situation, a young female australopithecine suddenly appears out of the

Heir apparent
Bruiser is a full grown male australopithecine. With no other competition, it is only a matter of time before he takes over from Greybeard.

One of the girls
Adolescent females move between groups and, although the males can be quick to accept a newcomer, it can often take her much longer to find a place among the other females.

Our feminine side

Chimps behaving badly
Jane Goodall's studies of chimps revealed they were male-dominated societies where killing, violence and even waging war were common.

Sexy beasts
Unlike their close cousins the chimps, in bonobo society females are dominant and, instead of aggression, sex is used to re-enforce hierarchies.

All palaeontologists look to the behaviour of modern animals to give a guide to that of extinct ones, and this is true of those studying our ancestors, too.

As Jane Goodall's work with chimpanzees in the wild revealed more and more about their social structure and behaviour, it seemed that their lives mirrored our own in many more ways than had previously been understood. Inevitably, conclusions started to be drawn about 'man's natural state' and hence about how our ancestors might have behaved. Chimpanzees are far from being the peaceful vegetarians they were once thought to be. Instead, Jane Goodall's study group showed that the males were often extremely violent – sometimes even systematically waging war on neighbouring groups. Parallels were easy to draw – men were 'naturally dominant' over women, and our ancestors were born killers.

However, chimpanzees have another very close relative – the bonobo, whose behaviour is utterly different. Although this was acknowledged in the 1930s and '40s, it was not widely reported – partly because it was often considered 'too shocking'.

Although they have the same basic social structure as chimps, the males are dominated by the females, and, although they are generally bigger and stronger, would never physically challenge or attack a female.

It was their attitude to sex which was found so shocking by the earlier scientists. Bonobos not only mate face to face, like humans, but they perform sex in every conceivable position and with every possible partner combination. For them, sex is not just for procreation, or even just for pleasure; they use it to decrease aggression within the group, for reassurance, to form political bonds and simply as a sign of affection.

Bonobos and chimpanzees are equally closely related to us, and yet exhibit very different social structures, showing how difficult it is to reconstruct the behaviour of our own ancestors.

bushes below and climbs the tree opposite. She does not attempt to come too close, but it is clear that she is making overtures to join the group. This is quite normal – when females reach maturity they often swap groups, which helps to maintain genetic diversity and prevent inbreeding. The group pretend to ignore her, but in truth she is being closely watched. Soon Greybeard clambers down from the tree and walks across to investigate the newcomer. Like all females who move between groups she has just become fertile and is very submissive. Greybeard mates with her, but this does not mean she has been accepted. She will have to learn the politics here and ingratiate herself with the other females before she can groom and feed with them.

Later in the afternoon the group are moving through the woodland and come across a recently killed ancylotherium, probably the work of the local dinofelis. Vultures and foxes are already fighting over what the cat has left behind. It is

When females reach maturity they often swap groups, helping to maintain genetic diversity and prevent inbreeding

known for australopithecines to eat carrion, but they are very choosy about it – they will not touch anything that has been dead for any length of time, probably because of the danger of contamination. They like to see it being killed. However, on this occasion, Greybeard decides to go and investigate, picking up a stick and chasing the vultures away. Meanwhile Bruiser takes the opportunity to mate with the new female. He makes no attempt to conceal what he is doing and it amounts to a direct challenge to Greybeard.

Greybeard comes charging back towards the group, dragging his stick after him and screaming at Bruiser. All the females scatter, but Bruiser stands his ground and the two males draw up to their full heights and start to chest each other. The whole group are screeching as Bruiser breaks off, climbs into a nearby tree and vigorously shakes the branches at Greybeard. The older ape then starts to lob stones at his rival. Unusually, there is no sign that either male is going to back down quickly. For all his bravado Greybeard knows that Bruiser is younger, larger and stronger than he is – the writing is on the wall. Suddenly Bruiser leaps down from the tree and charges Greybeard, knocking him to the ground. This seems to be a turning point. Greybeard does not get up quickly and when he does he seems more reluctant to challenge Bruiser. For the first time in seven years he tastes defeat. It is the end of an era and Greybeard has to acknowledge that the group now belongs to Bruiser.

Final showdown
Bruiser finally stands up to Greybeard's intimidation and, in a brief but violent encounter, Greybeard is defeated. Bruiser now becomes the dominant male.

Home security The next day Bruiser is once again mating with the new female. Although it will take several weeks for her to be fully accepted by the females of the group, the process is much quicker with the dominant male. It is still quite early in the morning and, unable to find any fruit among the pod mahogany, the group have moved to a more open area to dig for corkwood roots. Australopithecines are highly versatile foragers and this is partly because of their teeth. Although they have lost the long canines of other apes,

In another sign of their versatility, they have learned to use objects such as stones and sticks to help them dig

such as baboons, they have evolved thicker enamel. This allows them to cope with tougher vegetation and grit in their diet. So instead of just eating fruit, leaves and flowers they can also tackle highly nutritious roots and tubers. Of course most animals that specialize in buried food have specially adapted limbs for digging. The australopithecines' hands and arms seem unsuitable since they are designed to clamber among the branches. But, in another sign of their versatility, they have learned to use objects such as stones and sticks to help them dig. The dextrous hands and stereoscopic vision they developed in the trees are ideal for helping them wield tools.

Blue watches Babble as she chips away at the hard earth with a sharp stick. Occasionally she stops to sniff the hole she is making to check whether she is on the right track to find a corkwood root. Babble's baby plays round Blue, jumping up at him and then backing away in the hope that he will rise to the taunts. But, although Blue is much more accepted now, he has learned to moderate his behaviour, especially after the last beating he took from Babble.

A short distance away the mongooses are taking dry baths, slowly filling the clearing with a fine cloud of dust. As usual one of their number

Sticks and stones
Australopithecines are intelligent animals that can use tools to help them find food, especially nutrient-rich roots and tubers.

Mankind's cradle

New focus

In 1974, Johanson discovered the remains of a female australopithecine in northern Ethiopia. However, before more exensive research in the area could be carried out, civil war closed the region to science.

The scientific search for the metaphorical Garden of Eden took early fossil hunters across the face of the globe. Germany, England, Israel and Java were all considered to be candidates until, in 1924, the biologist Raymond Dart discovered the 2-million-year-old skeleton of a child in Taung, South Africa. Dart named it *Australopithecus africanus* and it was by far the oldest known hominid fossil. The search for human origins was instantly focused on Africa.

Through the next half century a number of significant fossil human finds were made across eastern and southern Africa, but although the finds were exciting no one discovered a hominid older than *Australopithecus africanus*. We were no

When assembled the bones formed the semi-complete skeleton of an adult woman whom Johanson named 'Lucy', after the song 'Lucy in the Sky with Diamonds'

nearer to finding the mythical Cradle of Human Evolution.

Throughout the early 1970s a series of finds were made around Lake Turkana in northern Kenya and then just over the border in southern Ethiopia. The

geographical range of the early hominids was being moved ever further north. The breakthrough came in 1974 when an expedition led by Don Johanson, fossil hunting in the remote Hadar region of northern Ethiopia, found a series of hominid bones that turned out to be our oldest known relative. When assembled the bones formed the semi-complete skeleton of an adult woman whom Johanson named 'Lucy', after the song 'Lucy in the Sky with Diamonds'. She turned out to be 3.2 million years old.

Life of grind
The teeth of early hominids show they had a mixed diet of fruit and leaves. Wear and tear from grit suggests they also ate roots.

Family dynasty
For decades the Leakey family pioneered research into early hominids in areas like Lake Turkana in northern Kenya.

Most importantly, her hips proved that she would have walked upright like ourselves and yet many of her features, such as the fingers and thorax, were essentially ape-like. Lucy was heralded as the missing link between humans and apes.

However, before any further discoveries could be made, a fierce civil war erupted in Ethiopia, closing the region to science for 20 years. When the palaeontologists were allowed back in they promptly found more first-class fossils, in both the southern and the northern regions of the country. In early 2001 it was reported that an older and more complete skeleton than Lucy's had been found near Hadar, confirming Ethiopia as a major centre for hominid evolution.

Ethiopia is far from most people's idea of a Garden of Eden, given that it contains one of the harshest deserts in the world. It is a wonder our tree-loving ancestors liked it so much. But the fossils show that back then the region was covered in a mixture of open forest and grassland, with intermittent lakes and rivers. There was also plenty of other wildlife of roughly the same type as can be seen in the African game parks today. To our ancestors, it would have been idyllic. In short, it was paradise in Lucy's day.

Famous find
It may not seem much, but the completeness of Lucy's skeleton was a revelation: there was enough evidence in her hips to prove she walked upright.

177

is on look-out and he is the first to spot the stalking dinofelis. In the bright, dusty light the cat's camouflage is ideal, but he has a lot of ground to cover to reach the australopithecines and once the mongoose sentry has spotted him he loses the element of surprise. Abandoning their digging, the group scramble for the nearest trees. Blue is the last to make it off the ground, with the dinofelis arriving a split second behind. The cat knows he has missed his chance, but that doesn't stop him stalking round the tree where Blue and four more of the group are hiding. Suddenly he plants his claws in the bough and drags himself up on to the lower branches. The apes scream in fear as the cat looks around for a way to climb higher.

Babble, Berry and Blue start to shake the branches and throw sticks. The cat ignores these threats as he makes ready to leap higher. However, just as he is about to jump, a particularly heavy branch from Babble hits him on the head. This makes him lose his balance and he falls out of the tree. The only thing that is hurt is his pride, but his humiliation seems to galvanize the terrified apes. As the females continue to throw things at him, Greybeard drops to the ground nearby and starts throwing stones. Not to be outdone, Bruiser appears with a large branch and charges, stopping short of the cat and screaming while he beats the ground. At first the predator slashes at Bruiser, but the sustained onslaught by the entire group eventually becomes too much and he is forced to retreat.

The females hoot and drum the branches while Bruiser continues to run forward, thumping the ground with his stick long after the cat has

> **Suddenly he plants his claws in the bough and drags himself up on to the lower branches. The apes scream in fear as the cat looks around for a way to climb higher**

Turning the tables
By acting together and using sticks and stones, the australopithecine group can defend themselves from even the biggest cat.

disappeared. It is a significant victory for the group and with any luck will make the dinofelis think twice before attacking again.

As the group calm down they gather in one tree and enjoy an extensive grooming session. For first time Babble lets Blue groom her and her baby. It has been a very close thing for Blue and he still looks much thinner than he should, but he is now interwoven in the social fabric of the group. He may never grow large enough to be the dominant male but, among these very complex creatures, every member of the group has its place and with luck Blue will occupy his for another forty years.

Happy families (OVERLEAF)
Under Bruiser's leadership the group establishes a new territory and Blue can finally be more sure of his future.

Our world 1 million years ago

The ice ages have arrived. Both North and South Poles are gripped in ice and thousands of square kilometres of tundra wilderness cloak the higher latitudes. This has driven much of life towards the Equator, but here another change awaits. With all the water locked up in the ice-caps, the tropics are drying out. Vast seas of grass now dominate the land. Nowhere is this change more obvious than in South America, where this period is known as the Pampean era. The rainforests have been pushed back to the coasts and replaced by open savanna and prairies. Here, the battle between predator and prey is intense – with no forests, there is little opportunity for games of hide and seek. This competition has bred a race of giants. Many are too large for the traditional top predators of South America, the flightless terror birds, but a new migrant from North America is changing the balance of power. The newcomers are called smilodon – they are sabre-toothed cats, and in South America they are the new terrors of the plains.

Girls on top (PREVIOUS PAGES) A group of female smilodon watch a herd of macrauchenia, waiting for the right moment to attack.

Ruler of the pride It is a scene as old as time on these Pampean plains. Ripples of wind chase across a sea of deep grass. In the distance a vast herd of macrauchenia move through the morning haze. Just visible above the waving seed heads is the dark plumage of a phorusrhacos out hunting mammals. For millions of years this huge terror bird and his kind have been the top predators in South America and they have grown large and powerful on it – this one is almost 3 metres (10 feet) tall. Terror birds are lightning-fast creatures, capable of speeds over 60 kilometres (37 miles) an hour; few herbivores here have the pace to escape them.

The phorusrhacos has crouched low, using the tall grass to hide in while he watches his unwitting victim wander nearer and nearer across some open ground. He slowly cocks his head from side to side to judge the precise moment to strike, his fearsome hooked beak held slightly open in anticipation. The little mammal he is watching stops, perhaps sensing

Phorusrhacos

Phorusrhacos belongs to a group called the terror birds, the earliest known of which, *Aenigmavis*, is actually found in the Messel deposits of Germany (see pages 56–7), but was only the size of a modern chicken and not related to the giant *Gastornis* which dominated the forests of the Eocene. However, in South America *Aenigmavis*'s descendants grew huge and became the continent's top predators for millions of years.

EVIDENCE: Only partial fossils of *Phorusrhacos* have been found, such as those at Monte Hermoso in Argentina, but recent finds of its North American form, *Titanis*, in Texas and Florida, are beginning to complete the picture.

SIZE: Almost 3 metres (10 feet) tall.

DIET: Small mammals and any carcasses it could find.

TIME: 27 million–5000 years ago.

Ancient terror

On the island continent of South America, flightless predatory birds thrived long after becoming extinct elsewhere. None was more spectacular than phorusrhacos.

185

Empty lands

Heart of grass
With the onset of the ice ages, the Amazon rainforest retreated to the coast and South America was dominated by grasslands.

The end of the Pliocene era saw the demise of the forest world that had dominated the life of mammals since the death of the dinosaurs. Although the climate was still warm in the mid-latitudes and the tropics, both ice-caps were expanding rapidly, creating a distinctive polar region around the Arctic and Antarctic. For the first time in nearly 300 million years, Earth had large areas of barren, frozen desert called tundra across the extreme northern regions of America, Europe and Asia and in the southern region of Patagonia. Grasslands thrived in these conditions, creating steppes, savannas and pampas, while tropical forests gave way to open woodland. The world was starting to look very much as it does today.

Such radical changes in climate and vegetation had a severe effect on the animal life of the planet. The tundra and polar conifer forest provided poor pickings for all but the most hardy of birds, mammals and insects. The warmer grasslands encouraged an explosion in the number of grass-eating rodents, rabbits and hares, which may in turn have caused an increase in medium-sized carnivores such as foxes, dogs and small cats. In the warmer forested parts of southern Europe the first mammoths emerged, although at this stage they were hairless and eating foliage rather than grass.

But the most significant developments were taking place on the tropical and subtropical grasslands of Africa, Asia and North America. Here the decline of the woodlands allowed hoofed animals such as horses, cows and antelope to expand on to the plains. The open spaces and plentiful grass supplies caused them to multiply into vast herds capable of

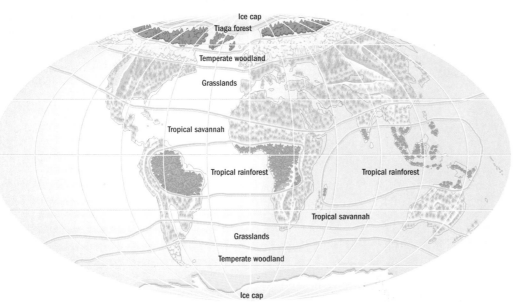

Ice cap
Tiaga forest
Temperate woodland
Grasslands
Tropical savannah
Tropical rainforest
Tropical rainforest
Tropical savannah
Grasslands
Temperate woodland
Ice cap

The freeze begins
By 1 million years ago the ice ages were well underway. As the ice caps expand at the poles, the tiaga forests spread towards the Equator, squeezing the other vegetation zones and almost eliminating the tropical rainforests. With so much water tied up in the poles, dry zones round the globe increased. As before, grass took over open areas even in the frozen north. This put pressure on older tropical animals, but it opened up vast new areas to those creatures that could adapt to cold, dry habitats.

Rain dancers (LEFT)
In Africa, the huge migrations of herds which follow the rains probably started with the climate changes of the ice ages.

Masked migrant (RIGHT)
Relatives of the raccoons were some of the first animals to move from North to South America.

migrating with the seasonal rains. In response to this abundant food source came the fleet-footed large cats, such as leopards and lions, which were fast enough to hunt on the plains.

Another feature of this time was the mixing of different animal populations because of the low sea levels. Asian animals such as elephants and cats moved into North America, and African fauna into southern Europe. Perhaps the most notable mixing occurred in South America. Here, because of their long isolation, the animals had responded to the clearing of the

forests in their own unique way. The pampas was filled with giant glyptodont armadillos and ground sloths. With these giants came some unlikely top predators, most notably the terror birds, which could

With these giants came some unlikely top predators, most notably the terror birds, which could run and hunt as effectively as the big cats

run and hunt as effectively as the big cats elsewhere. But then, about 3 million years ago, having been disconnected since the Jurassic, the two Americas crashed together. Animals started to wander back and forth. The South gave Texas and Florida their sloths, armadillos and terror birds. The North gave Argentina raccoons, rodents and sabre-toothed cats.

Only Australia remained isolated from all other continents, as it had done for 45 million years, but even here the grasslands were spreading – to the advantage of the fast-moving kangaroos.

Adult

Cub

Smilodon

Smilodon, the famous sabre-toothed cat, is well known because of the enormous numbers of skeletons of the North American species, *Smilodon fatalis*, which are beautifully preserved in the tar pits of La Brea in California. The South American species, *Smilodon populator*, was even larger than its North American cousin with long, strong front legs to hold down prey and to get an accurate bite with the sabre teeth.

EVIDENCE: *Smilodon populator* is known from several sites in Brazil, Argentina and especially the Tarija formation in Bolivia.

SIZE: 1.2 metres (4 feet) at the shoulder.

DIET: Large grazing or browsing animals.

TIME: 1.5 million–100,000 years ago.

Fragile safety

Young smilodon cubs are safe within the pride as long as food is not in short supply and the dominant male is not usurped.

danger, and calls out for help. The phorusrhacos stands up and charges on swift orange legs. But he is in for a surprise.

The terror bird's victim is a smilodon cub, a baby sabre-tooth, and, although the little creature has wandered out on his own, there will be a pride nearby. The sheer pace of the terror bird means he is on to the cub before any help can arrive, but the youngster's stumbling retreat stops the predator making a clean grab. As he rounds on his victim, the phorusrhacos finds himself facing a full-grown mother smilodon, her mouth wide open to reveal her enormous 20-centimetre (8-inch) fangs. The giant bird spreads his small, clawed wings in a defiant display, issuing a piercing screech of aggression. But this impressive sight fails to intimidate the huge sabre-tooth. She lunges forward, lashing with her claws and placing herself between the cub and the bird. Soon two more female smilodon appear out of the grass and then a huge lumbering male. The phorusrhacos is now way out of his league. When the male smilodon breaks into a trot, the terror bird turns and runs. The big cat knows better than to pursue him. Instead, he stops and issues a series of low, throaty roars that rumble across the plains after the retreating bird. His calls are cut short when a playful cub sinks its teeth into the male's short tail and he has to turn and cuff it free.

A smilodon's roar can carry for 8 kilometres (5 miles) across the savanna and serves not only as a warning to other predators, but also as a reminder to the other smilodon prides. To the sabre-toothed cats this sea of grass is a giant chequerboard of territories, each defended by a pride. The size of each area depends on the wealth of prey that can be found there and the health of the pride that controls it. This particular pride is not large. Five females with four cubs and two adolescent females are dominated by a single male. Their territory stretches for several kilometres along the base of a cliff and contains mostly grassland, with a few stands of palms and patches of seasonal marshland.

Rattling sabres

Domestic killers
Cats attack prey smaller than themselves with teeth that are primarily designed to break little bones.

The phrase 'sabre-toothed' immediately conjures up the word 'tiger' in most people's minds, but sabre teeth have evolved at least four times in mammals – and not once in a tiger. There have been sabre-toothed cats (such as *Smilodon*), but also sabre-toothed marsupials, and other sabre-toothed cat-like animals – the extinct nimravids and creodonts.

Some small cats kill their prey with a carefully placed bite to the back of their victim's neck, which is neatly broken by the predator's canine teeth. At first glance this would seem a good explanation for the sabre teeth: large cats, killing large prey, have large canines with which to break their victims' necks. But there's a problem. The sabres are actually quite delicate – any contact with bone and they would shatter.

Many large cats, such as lions, strangle their prey by biting its throat and holding the

Famous gape
Long sabre teeth evolved again and again in predatory mammals and are thought to help specifically with killing larger prey.

windpipe closed. This would seem a better way to use sabre teeth. With an accurate bite, the sabres would have accelerated the death of the prey. As the cat closed its mouth on the neck of its victim, the sabre teeth could have punctured the major blood vessels to the brain, as well as closing off the windpipe, quickly killing the animal. However, for this to work, the cat had to be able to subdue the struggling prey, so that it did not put its delicate teeth at risk.

Smilodon had several adaptations which may have helped it kill in this way. First, it had very powerful forelegs with permanently sharp retractable claws, which would have helped it bring its prey to the ground and hold it still so as to get an accurate bite. Then its skull shows a very large nerve supply to its whiskers, which would have helped it find exactly the right place to bite, just as modern cats' whiskers do. Finally, its row of front teeth stuck out slightly, allowing it to strip meat from the carcass without its sabre teeth getting in the way. The wear patterns on *Smilodon*'s teeth show that it avoided bone almost entirely – probably to protect its huge sabres – with the result that it would have left plenty of meat for the scavengers on the plains.

The male took over this 'cliff' pride almost two years ago by killing the previous male. He is a fine example of his species, standing about a metre and a half-tall with massively powerful front limbs. His relatively short back legs and stubby tail mean that he moves a bit like a hyaena. So, although he cannot run fast, he can keep up a sustained canter if needed. However, it is not his job actually to hunt. The females do all the killing; he just claims his share when they are successful, saving his strength for challenges to the pride, mainly from other males. But this male has not faced a serious challenge for his territory – as yet his sandy, spotted hide has few scars. Despite this, one of his long sabre canines is broken halfway down. This does not appear to impede him, but it does make him easily recognizable.

As the pride settles down again after their run-in with the phorusrhacos, the half-toothed male relaxes on top of some open rock with the females and cubs around him. Before him, stretching away from the cliff, are his pride lands, which contain several herds of the small horse-like creatures known as hippidiforms, and macrauchenia. The macrauchenia are large herbivores with characteristically long noses that they use to help gather food. Because they are comparatively slow-moving they are the smilodon's favourite prey, but no creature here is easy meat. These are large, powerful herbivores and it is very difficult to isolate individuals from the herd.

Half Tooth rolls over and lets a cub bat his ears. All the cubs here are his and most are just a few months old. They are more heavily speckled than the adults and have yet to develop their sabre teeth. It is a picture of family peace, the king of the plains surrounded by his subjects. But there is trouble on his horizon. Across the endless plains wander the unmistakable shapes of two large male smilodon. They are brothers and, although they are strangers to this area, they have deliberately ignored the frequent scenting points that Half Tooth has left around his territory. They are here to challenge him and will not leave until there has been bloodshed.

Defence of the realm
Half Tooth roars in the evening light. Most of his energy is spent marking and defending his territory.

Doedicurus

Doedicurus was a glyptodont, related to modern armadillos and to the sloths. It did very well in South America long after disappearing everywhere else. When a land link with North America formed, *Doedicurus* continued to thrive but eventually succumbed with the rest of the megafauna. Legends suggest that they were still alive when humans first arrived in South America, but these may be based purely on their impressive remains.

EVIDENCE: Many skeletons of glyptodonts are known, including those of *Doedicurus*, especially in the Esenada formation in Argentina.

SIZE: 3 metres (10 feet) long, weighing around 1.4 tonnes.

DIET: Browsed and grazed any vegetation it could find, possibly digging for roots and tubers as well.

TIME: 2 million–15,000 years ago.

The king is banished The next morning the sun rises into a dark, overcast sky. By late morning the rain is drenching the plains. Beneath the dripping leaves of a palm grove are the dark brown shapes of two huge male doedicurus, battling for the right to mate a nearby female. It is an extraordinary trial of strength for these huge armoured creatures. Their rigid, domed bodies make them look slow and clumsy as they manoeuvre round each other, seeking an opportunity to strike. They push and shove, grunt and bark, even occasionally rising up on their back legs to try and intimidate their rival. Then one will manage to land a blow with his massive spiked tail. When 40 kilograms (90 pounds) of bony club smash into thick body armour cushioned by layers of fat, it produces a sickening thud. A fine spray of water leaps off the rivals' backs as the shock of the blow vibrates round their carapaces. But each time the victim just grunts and the fight continues. Sometimes these bludgeoning contests last for hours and individuals walk away comparatively unscathed, broken spikes or cracked armour being the worst injuries. It looks as if, despite the rain, this encounter is also going to last.

From a nearby mound the 'cliff' pride watches the contest with detachment. It is unlikely that either doedicurus will be so weakened as to

The giant glyptodont armadillos evolved all sorts of armoured tails, similar to those of the ancient ankylosaur dinosaurs, but none was as spectacular as the spiked club of doedicurus.

Trial of strength
Doedicurus males fight over a female. The rules are simple: the winner is the one who can stand being bashed the longest.

make him vulnerable to attack. Besides, the females are distracted.
At dawn the two brothers stood about a kilometre (half a mile) from the
pride, issuing challenging calls. Half Tooth responded by trotting off into
the long grass to find them. He has not been seen since. The females
need to hunt, but they are worried about leaving their cubs. Eventually,
around midday, Half Tooth appears out of the rain. He is covered in mud
and limping. The adults in the pride stand up to greet him, but as he
approaches it is clear he has several nasty wounds on his flanks. Then
through the mist come the two brothers. Their heads are up, they are
watching Half Tooth – just keeping pace so that he has no opportunity to
stop to rest. Outnumbered, he has lost his fight. He has been deposed and
now he is being driven from his former territory.

Smilodon's jaws are specially adapted to
open wider than most cats, allowing them to
sink their sabres into the neck of their prey.

The females start to call out, but Half Tooth skirts round the pride, heading for the swamps and palm forests to the south. His future looks bleak – few males last long after they have been ousted from their pride. With no territory to call his own and no females to hunt for him, he will be reduced to scavenging, rejected by other prides and attacked by other males. However, Half Tooth is still comparatively young and there is a slim chance that, if his wounds are not too bad, he might be able to make a comeback.

The two brothers give up the chase as Half Tooth disappears into the swampland. They then settle down to lick their wounds and watch their new pride from a safe distance. The females know what has happened – some have seen it twice in their lifetimes already. It is all change at the top. But although this makes little difference to them, it is lethal for their cubs. The brothers know that the youngsters belong to Half Tooth, and they are not about to protect his offspring. Also, as long as the cubs are

As far as the brothers are concerned, they must kill their defeated rival's young in order to mate with the females and sire cubs of their own

there, the females will not come into season. As far as the brothers are concerned, they must kill their defeated rival's young in order to mate with the females and sire cubs of their own. At first the brothers do not approach the pride – they know the cubs will be defended aggressively. But the mothers cannot stay by their babies for ever – they need to go hunting. Eventually, grasping their cubs delicately in their front teeth, they move off into some thorn scrub to hide them. The brothers are happy to wait.

By now Half Tooth has reached the open forest at the base of the cliffs. He is looking for shelter from the rain and heads for a large overhanging rock. Before he climbs up to the overhang he stops and sniffs the air.

Just distinguishable through the rain is the stench of the giant ground sloth, megatherium. This is the first piece of luck Half Tooth has had today. If he had blundered into an enclosed space with a 4-tonne megatherium he could well have been killed instantly. As it is, he turns and stalks up to high ground to the right of the overhang; sure enough, squatting among some myrtle, is the massive hulk of an adult megatherium. His dark, shaggy coat is soaked and his powerful clawed arms are lightly stripping palm leaves, leisurely feeding the greenery into his mouth. The lumbering beast spots the sabre-tooth and issues a roar. He rises up on his back legs, lifting his arms high in threat and displaying his claws, which are every bit as long as the cat's sabre teeth. Being so powerful, megatherium have little to fear, even from smilodon, but still they do not tolerate the cats anywhere near them.

Half Tooth is now in some pain. The bruises and wounds the brothers gave him are beginning to seize up in the damp atmosphere. Stumbling over the rocks he retreats from the dangerous sloth and continues his search for shelter.

Later that afternoon the brothers are completing Half Tooth's defeat. As the rains gradually ease off they get up and shake the water out of their coats. The females of the pride have gone hunting and the brothers head for the thorn scrub. It may be that they won't find the cubs today, but in the end it will make no difference. Every time the females have to leave their young, the brothers will try to find them and eventually they will succeed.

Just before darkness the pride females return and the mothers search for their cubs. Their low calls go unanswered. The mothers continue searching into the night, but without success – it would appear that the brothers are efficient hunters. The oldest female keeps looking for her two cubs for several days. She is probably too old to have another litter and perhaps she is aware that this is her last chance. Three days after Half Tooth was deposed, she discovers the severed head of one of her babies.

Bully of the plains
The power and size of the giant ground sloth megatherium mean that he faces no natural predators on the pampas.

Megatherium
The ground sloths, although related to the tree sloths, were very different from their modern relatives. They grew to enormous sizes – *Megatherium* being one of the largest – and successfully crossed from South America into North America, where they did equally well. Ground sloths became extinct only a few thousand years ago, possibly due to hunting by humans, and so there is still quite a lot of evidence of what they looked like.

EVIDENCE: The South American species *Megatherium americanum* is known from many skeletons, sets of fossilized footprints and even dung and hair. Finds have come from as far north as Texas and as far south as Argentina.

SIZE: Up to 6 metres (20 feet) long, weighing around 3.8 tonnes.

DIET: Browsed vegetation, and possibly scavenged meat from carcasses.

TIME: 1.9 million–8000 years ago.

Macrauchenia

This bizarre-looking creature is a member of a group of extinct animals called litopterns, known only from South America. No one knows how they are related to other mammals – they are assumed to be distant relatives of our familiar hoofed mammals, but this classification may change when more fossils are found. *Macrauchenia* was the last of its kind – when it became extinct the litoptern lineage died with it.

EVIDENCE: The first *Macrauchenia* skeleton was discovered by Charles Darwin on a stop-over during his famous journey on board *The Beagle*. Since then many more remains have been found in the Lujan formation in Argentina.

SIZE: 2.1 metres (7 feet) at the shoulder. Over 3 metres (10 feet) tall at head height.

DIET: Browsed on trees.

TIME: 7 million–20,000 years ago.

New regime Across the Pampean grasslands, the weeks of heavy rain have left the ground waterlogged. Temporary pools lie hidden beneath a lush growth of new grass and for the herbivores there is no shortage of food. However, the soft heavy soil is bad news for many herd animals. Most, like the macrauchenia and the horses, rely on their speed and manoeuvrability to escape predators. The ground conditions now make this difficult – something the pride of smilodon know how to turn to its advantage.

The brothers still have little to do with the females and are probably waiting for the first one to come into season. Most of the time they wander their new territory, scent-marking to establish their presence. Meanwhile, four of the females are out hunting. The oldest one who lost her cubs is not among them. In fact, she has not been seen for a week and it is quite possible that she is dead. The other members of the pride will miss her experience, but she has taught them well and, in her absence, they are carefully organizing the death of yet another macrauchenia.

The macrauchenia herd have gathered in the open and are browsing in a mass of mimosa bushes. Normally these animals specialize in the shrubs and trees, using their extraordinary prehensile noses to pluck tasty leaves off branches. But in this time of plenty there is no need to work so hard and the flowers are an additional treat. As usual the herd is nervous. Even though these are powerful creatures, with some adults growing to over 3 metres (10 feet) tall, they know they are well matched by the hunting tactics of the sabre-toothed pride. As they move forward, plucking at the flowers, their heads bob up and down, scanning the horizon for danger. Of course, the smilodon are aware of this and so the four females are approaching with bellies almost scraping the ground, their muscular shoulders below the level of the grass. Through the blizzard of seed heads they keep a watchful eye on the movement of the herd.

Macrauchenia's distinctive 'hose-nose' has developed to help it browse on new growth on trees and bushes. At this level it faces less competition for food than if it relied on grass.

Herd mentality
Despite being the size of camels, macrauchenia are always alert to danger. They are the favourite prey of the sabre-toothed smilodon.

Three of the females work their way quickly to the east of the macrauchenia; the fourth moves to the west and settles down to wait. Soon the first three are in position. Very slowly they work their way closer and closer to the herd. There are several youngsters near them, but smilodon are one of the few cats that seem just as willing to take on healthy adults as they are to attack the more vulnerable targets such as the sick and the old.

The stalkers get to within 50 metres (160 feet) before they are spotted, then a male brays in alarm. His call is picked up by the rest of the herd and they start to gallop off towards the west. The three cats accelerate out of their hiding places. Quickly the lead female gains on a straggler but, just as she falls into step with it and prepares to strike, the macrauchenia lurches away from her. The cat stumbles as she tries to change direction and, by the time she has recovered, her victim has gained a precious 10 metres (30 feet). This extraordinary agility for such a large creature is what has saved many a macrauchenia. Unfortunately not this one. Its change of direction takes it away from the herd and right in front of the hidden fourth smilodon. It takes only a couple of strides to bring the cat beside her victim and, before it can react again, she strikes. She leaps on the herbivore's flanks, sinking her claws into its shoulders and neck. The weight and power of the smilodon topples the macrauchenia and both animals collapse into a shallow pond in a spray of muddy water.

The herbivore kicks vigorously, but the cat is careful to throw her body clear at the front end of her victim. Keeping one paw firmly on its shoulders, she tries to anchor its head with the other. A second huntress arrives and together the two cats hold down the struggling prey. The first then opens her mouth enormously wide and clamps her sabre teeth on to

The cat stumbles as she tries to change direction and, by the time she has recovered, her victim has gained a precious 10 metres

When continents collide

South America's 30 million years as an island allowed animals to evolve into forms never seen in the rest of the world. Then, about 3 million years ago, after a series of tentative couplings, it finally docked with North America. It was once thought that the endemic fauna of South America, weakened by aeons of isolation, was overrun by the more robust fauna of North America. But scientists now realize that the answer is more complicated than that.

Green return
Climate change can clear rainforest more completely than humans, and the mighty Amazonian rainforest has come and gone many times.

The grasslands of South America had their ground sloths, glyptodonts and terror birds, as well as their own range of rodents and marsupials. When the continent joined to North America, a corridor of grassland formed, allowing the plains-living animals of the two worlds to meet. Many South American animals moved into the southern plains of North America, but further north the climate became much colder, stopping them from spreading further afield.

North American animals also moved south into the new pastures, and had a greater expanse into which to spread. Horses, camels (the ancestors of the llamas of South America), deer and tapirs started to graze and browse on the plains, and brought with them new predators – the dogs and the cats, including the famous sabre-toothed cat, *Smilodon*.

About 2.5 million years ago, the climate began to warm up, and the Amazon rainforest crept in from the coasts to form a band across the land bridge between the Americas. The plains animals could no longer cross between the two continents, and the two became effectively isolated from each other again. The climate fluctuated between warm and cool throughout the ice ages, putting a strain on the bigger animals. Large animals cannot

High planes drifter
Despite being an icon of the South American Andes, the llama is a comparative newcomer, having arrived from North America only 2–3 million years ago.

adapt to fast-changing conditions, as they reproduce slowly and have smaller population sizes, making them more prone to extinction. By the end of the final cool period, 12,000 years ago, many of the giants that had evolved in South America had become extinct or, at best, very rare. The last few ground sloths and even terror birds may have been around when humans first colonized the Americas, according to recent fossil finds. Many North American animals still thrive in South America. The South Americans are having a harder time adapting to the cooler North American climate, but a relative of the glyptodonts – the armadillo – is even now increasing its range every year as it evolves to withstand the cold winters of the north.

Two-pronged attack (OVERLEAF)
Having ambushed a macrauchenia, two smilodon wrestle their prey to the ground before delivering their lethal bites.

the macrauchenia's neck. Quickly she works her fangs deeper, eventually shearing through her victim's windpipe, oesophagus and arteries in one go. The kicking stops as the other two females arrive and the pride settles down to feed. To do this they tear at the flesh with their incisors or chew with their back teeth – their giant fangs are of no use while eating.

It is not long before the brothers appear to claim their share. On approach they bellow and roar to assert their authority. There is still a lot of tension within the pride, but even under normal circumstances the females would be reluctant to give up their prize. Scraps break out and there are a lot of threat displays, but inevitably the males eventually settle on the carcass. While they feed the others have to hold back or risk a raking blow. To make matters worse, other animals, such as vultures and foxes, have been attracted to the kill. More significantly, two phorusrhacos have also appeared. Although these giant birds will not challenge the pride directly, they frequently use their speed to dart in and steal food.

The smilodon always leave a lot on a carcass because they do not want to risk breaking their long sabre teeth on bones

For an hour the males jealously fend off challenges as they eat their fill. By the time the females are allowed to start eating again there are four phorusrhacos probing round the edges, as well as several smaller animals such as raccoons. They all know that the smilodon always leave a lot on a carcass because they do not want to risk breaking their long sabre teeth on bones. This gives the scavengers plenty to squabble over.

Over the next few weeks the females settle into the new regime. Food is plentiful and with no cubs to feed one of them soon comes into heat. The males have been waiting for this, although it is the female who makes the first approaches. She rolls over on her back in front of them to signal

Feeding frenzy
Smilodon's sabre teeth can be a hindrance whilst eating a kill, so its incisors have grown forwards, enabling it to strip meat from the bone.

her receptiveness. The immediate effect of this is to start a fight between the brothers. So far they have co-operated in everything, but only one can mate with the female and the decision has to be made with a show of force. This is something that pride males seem to be able to work out without injuring each other – next time it may be the other brother's turn. For now, the winner will spend the next three days escorting the female around their territory, mating regularly every hour.

In exile The ground is drying out after the rains. Most of the flowers have gone and the grass lies uninterrupted to the horizon. At the base of the cliffs a mother doedicurus is busy constructing a huge mound of brush and grass. This is her nest. She will not use it for long, because her babies have to learn to trot after her when they are quite young. But for at least the first few weeks she will stay in the nest, feeding them while their shells harden.

The mother doedicurus is being watched by Half Tooth. In the months since his defeat he has not moved far from his old territory. He has recovered from his wounds and is living the life of all solitary male smilodon. He must somehow survive alone while avoiding clashes with pride cats. Much of his day is spent checking the scent marks left by other dominant males round their territories. He is looking for any sign of weakness – anything that might encourage him to challenge an incumbent male. He also regularly checks the marks left by the brothers.

The terror bird leaps up and charges the herd – they scatter, but the speed of the predator means it is soon amongst them

His biggest problem is catching prey by himself. Smilodon are not fast and he is not a skilful stalker like the females of his species. After watching the busy doedicurus for some time he heads off towards a small herd of horses. They are quick, skittish animals and unless he is lucky he stands little chance of catching them off guard. However, he has noticed something else. A large phorusrhacos is crouched low in the grass and it has its eye on one of the smaller foals. About 100 metres (330 feet) from the horses the terror bird leaps up and charges the herd – they scatter, but the speed of the predator means it is soon amongst them. It is concentrating on one mother and her young. Despite their best attempts to side-step the feathered monster, it succeeds in snatching at the foal's back legs, sending it tumbling away from its mother. The phorusrhacos quickly pins the little horse down

The beak of the giant terror bird phorusrhacos is subtly different from the crushing hatchet of gastornis. It is closer to that of modern raptors, such as the eagle, and is ideal for tearing meat.

Sharing the spoils

A pair of phorusrhacos fight for the carcass of a small hippidiform horse.

with its clawed feet. The mother stops a short distance away. She is powerless to drive the predator from her panicked youngster. However, its pain is short-lived – the bird's huge beak soon breaks its neck. Immediately the predator is joined by a second terror bird and they start to fight over the carcass.

All this is observed by Half Tooth, who has been slowly trotting after the hunting terror bird. The phorusrhacos have not had a chance to take more than a couple of mouthfuls of their meal before the sabre-tooth makes his challenge. This is what he is good at – chasing other predators off their prey, even if it is usually female smilodon. He roars and displays his fangs. One bird tries to lift the carcass and run away with it, but the foal is too heavy. After a lot of indignant screeching the phorusrhacos have to back off and the cat has the foal to himself. Today is a good day for Half Tooth.

The regime cracks After several months of baking heat the plains have dried out. The palms stand out like green islands in a sea of yellow grass. A trail of dust betrays the mother doedicurus digging for roots. Her three pink youngsters stand nearby, flicked with dirt. She has only recently abandoned her nest, but her offspring are now mobile enough, and their skins hard enough, to resist attack at least from small predators. However, they still need their mother to see off monsters such as the phorusrhacos.

For the moment the local terror birds are distracted by a smilodon hunt. The 'cliff' pride have just brought down a large macrauchenia and the phorusrhacos are, as usual, waiting their turn. The pride is at full strength and, although there are no cubs yet, the brothers have mated with most of the females. They are now feeding and the males sit apart, licking their blood-spattered fur. Things seem to have settled down well for the new regime, but everything is about to change.

The kill is not far from the trees at the base of the cliff. With the dry weather, food has become scarce for all the animals here, including the

Dust bath
A herd of macrauchenia roll in the dirt. This behaviour helps them control skin parasites.

local megatherium. There are several of these shaggy creatures living in the open forests above and below the cliffs, and one has smelt the smilodon kill. Normally these giant sloths survive happily on a varied diet of leaves, bark and roots, but in exceptional circumstances they will scavenge meat. And when a megatherium decides it wants something, there is nothing on the Pampean plains that can stop it.

Slowly, through the shimmering heat, the ground sloth wanders towards the pride, stopping occasionally to sniff the air. The brothers notice him first and jump to their feet. They start calling and the females round the carcass stop feeding. As the sloth gets closer he rises up on his back legs to make himself look even more impressive. He responds to the males' challenge with his own gruff roar.

The females are now nervous and back away from the body. The brothers, however, stand their ground, perhaps hoping the sloth will

continue on past their hard-earned meal. But he continues straight towards them with his weird shuffling gait. The smilodon make fake runs at him, their hackles raised and their sabres flashing. But it is all to no effect – he just keeps coming. Suddenly one male slips in a dust pocket and ends up sprawled in front of the giant sloth. With deceptive speed and power the megatherium strikes out with his long arms. The smilodon yelps in pain as the sloth's claws find their mark. He rolls back, but the sloth ambles forward and brings his claws crashing down again. The sabre-tooth drops on to his side, helpless, and the enraged sloth pummels him until he stops moving.

By now the rest of the pride, including the other brother, have retired some distance away. The sloth drags at the male's limp body, then shuffles on to the macrauchenia carcass. He sits down next to it and, using his massive forearms to tear its side open, starts to feed. The pride ends up about a kilometre away and can only sit and watch. The brother is alone, probably for the first time in his life, and he is going to find it twice as difficult to defend his territory from other males – including Half Tooth.

Just before nightfall the megatherium moves on and smaller scavengers, including six phorusrhacos, seize their chance. Although there is not much left on the macrauchenia carcass, there is the bonus of an untouched male smilodon body nearby.

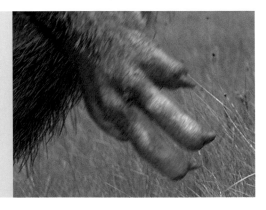

Of all the weapons on the Pampean plains, a megatherium's claws are perhaps the most fearsome. Although designed for pulling down branches and stripping bark, they can equally kill a sabre-tooth with one blow.

No contest
When a giant megatherium decides to supplement its diet with some scavenged meat, even the mighty sabre-toothed cats have to back down.

The mother of all sloths

The giant ground sloths must be one of the most extraordinary mammals ever to have lived and, frustratingly, they were still roaming the Americas until a few thousand years ago. In other words, to the palaeontologist of the future they are our contemporaries. The first skeleton was found at the end of the eighteenth century in what is now Argentina. It was sent back to Madrid and correctly identified as an edentate, meaning toothless – a group of animals that includes the sloths, armadillos and anteaters. The drawings of this specimen were seen by the American

These animals regularly walked upright on their hind legs. Indeed, most of the trackways so far discovered are from ground sloths walking on two legs

president Thomas Jefferson, who realized that this was a very similar animal to one that had been found in Virginia, USA, which he had originally thought was a giant lion. Beautifully preserved specimens of several species of ground sloth were also beginning to be found in the tar pits of Rancho La Brea, California.

Among the commonest fossils found in the La Brea tar pits are pebble-like dermal ossicles, tiny bones which are embedded in the skin. A cave in South America has

Rival of the dinosaurs
One of the most noticeable things about the *Megatherium* skeleton is how massive the bones are; big enough to be compared with dinosaurs.

Clownish relative (ABOVE)
Looking at modern tree sloths, it is hard to imagine how impressive the giant ground sloth must have been.

Footprints in time (LEFT)
Magnificently preserved footprints show the giant sloth walked upright, supporting its weight on the side of its feet.

preserved the mummified skin of a ground sloth, and this shows that the ossicles formed a complete set of 'chain mail' in the skin, making the animal almost impervious to predators' claws or teeth. But it has not all been bones. Dry caves in south-western USA have also preserved the huge claws,

and large amounts of ground sloth dung, so we know precisely what ground sloths in that area were eating. Some 72 species of plant were identified from this dung, so it seems they were not fussy.

Fossil *Megatherium* trackways have also been found and it would appear that

these animals regularly walked upright on their hind legs. Indeed, most of the trackways so far discovered are from ground sloths walking on two legs. The giant sloths must have weighed almost 4 tonnes, and so walking on two legs would have put a tremendous strain on their skeletons. What is more, the prints are shaped like a comma, with a ridge of mud pushed away from the outside edge, showing that they walked on the edges of their feet, with their toes curled inwards, as anteaters do today. Just why such huge giants would walk like this is a mystery. If only they had hung on a few thousand more years we might have been able to answer this question in a wildlife film.

Long live the king Several months have passed since Half Tooth was ousted by the brothers and he has done comparatively well on his own. He has avoided too many damaging confrontations with other sabre-tooths and has hunted or scavenged enough to remain strong and fit. In the last few weeks he has picked up a change in the scenting patterns left by the surviving brother. For the first time he has started leaving his own scent marks in his old territory as a challenge. As each day passes he grows bolder, moving further and further into the 'cliff' pride's land.

The females of the pride are unaware of this. They are all resting in the shade of some palms about 2 kilometres (1.5 miles) from the cliff. All four are now pregnant. They watch as the mother doedicurus protects her young ones from a pair of phorusrhacos. One of the birds has managed to seize a squealing baby by the tail and is attempting to drag it somewhere where its lethal hooked beak can get to work on its victim's armoured skin. But the mother doedicurus is having none of this and, with angry swishes of her enormous spiked tail, she charges back and forth after the birds. The phorusrhacos cannot afford to get their legs broken and they cannot outrun the doedicurus while they are carrying her heavy youngster. Eventually, after dropping the baby several times and picking it up again, the birds give up. Slightly blooded and very dirty, the young doedicurus returns to its mother's side.

Suddenly the male smilodon notices something else. About a kilometre (half a mile) away, Half Tooth has decided to make his presence very visible. It would be unusual for Half Tooth to regain his old pride, but with the death of one of the brothers the balance of power has shifted enormously. Not only that, but Half Tooth is slightly larger than the surviving male.

The challenger moves off towards a small valley full of alder and willow where is a water hole. The brother issues a series of low threatening roars, but Half Tooth does not respond. He knows he has been seen, but he does

Old enemies
Having evolved under the reign of the terror birds, doedicurus is completely immune to their attack.

6 A Mammmoth's Journey

Our world 30,000 years ago

All the signs are that this is one of the worst ice ages yet. For over a million years our world has suffered from a volatile and unpredictable climate. At the tropics, although the temperatures are more consistent, the forests keep advancing and retreating, driven by the changes in rainfall. Towards the poles it is a different story, especially in the north. With each ice age the ice caps spread across the continents, grinding the landscape with their glaciers and creating vast areas of dry, cold tundra and steppe. Yet, astonishingly, life has evolved to exploit this grim environment. Grasses, sedges and a range of trees have adapted to take full advantage of the brief summers. Large herbivores such as bison and rhinoceros have grown thick woolly coats, and predators such as lions turn snowy white in winter to help them stalk unnoticed through the icy landscape. One creature above all has come to epitomize life's adaptability and refusal to abandon even the bleakest environment – the woolly mammoth. All across the northern continents thousands of herds of these ice-age giants harvest the grasslands under the shadow of the glaciers. It is a tough life, but these animals are born to it.

All together now (PREVIOUS PAGES) Mammoths usually move in small herds of eight or nine, but as they move north for summer grazing, they may combine into groups of thousands.

Mid August A low summer sun throws up shadows across the rolling hills of the steppe. It is a warm evening and the air is thick with undulating swarms of midges. Underfoot the vegetation is lush with a range of sedges, club moss and dwarf trees scrabbling for room among dense swards of grass. Here and there clumps of trees such as larch and alder grow in the valleys and in between them herds of bison, horse and reindeer graze. One day this whole area will be flooded by the North Sea, but for now it is rich summer pasture. However, this apparently benign landscape hides its true nature in summer colours. Just to the north lies a gigantic ice sheet and, in a few weeks, temperatures here will begin to plummet with the approach of a long ice-age winter. Only the hardiest plants can survive. Not only do they have to remain dormant and frozen during the many winter months, but even in the short summer bloom there is very little rain. Many of the animals here are not permanent residents; they are just summer visitors taking advantage of the new growth while they can.

Following the herds of herbivores every year are predators and scavengers. Beneath a long, low ridge, a group of one such animal, some humans, are picking over a reindeer carcass left by a pack of wolves. In the twilight their distinctive, guttural babble drifts across the valley as they concentrate on the task of stripping the animal of what meat the wolves have left behind. Their unique ability to use stone tools, developed from their ancient African ancestors, allows them to make the most of what is available. In fact their task is so absorbing that they fail to notice approaching danger.

> Many of the animals here are not permanent residents; they are just summer visitors taking advantage of the new growth while they can

Homo sapiens

Modern humans, whose skeletons are identical to our own, are first found in Europe around 40,000 years ago, having spread from the Middle East and North Africa. We have the remains of huts which they built, their spectacular carvings and paintings, and even jewellery. The carvings include human figures showing people wearing woven clothing, and there are also ritual burials where the body is covered in ivory beads which seem to have been sewn on to cloth which has since disintegrated.

EVIDENCE: Modern humans spread relatively rapidly across southern Europe from the Middle East, and left campsites, painted caves and tools as well as bones.

SIZE: Males 1.85 metres (6 feet) tall, females 1.7 metres (5 feet 6 inches).

DIET: Humans were very adaptable in what they ate. Certainly they ate fruit and vegetables as well as meat, but each campsite seems to show different favourite prey animals. Rabbits and hares were among the most popular. In one camp in Italy, though, the humans seem to have specialized in hunting tortoises!

TIME: About 100,000 years ago to the present day.

Deceptive beauty
Although they look beautiful, the barren grasslands and frozen forest near the poles are cruel places for animals and plants to survive in.

Life in the freezer

In the last few hundreds of thousands of years the Earth's climate has changed from that of a greenhouse to that of an icehouse. This so-called ice age is in fact a series of ice ages, about 20 major ones so far, with cycles of cold glacial periods alternating with warmer interglacials. The first full cycles lasted about 40,000 years, although by the time of the later ice ages they were taking about 100,000 years to complete. The annual temperature would fall only by a few degrees Celsius, but this

was enough to spread kilometre-thick ice sheets across the globe. In the northern hemisphere these reached as far south as London and New York, while separate sheets formed over high regions of the world such as the Andes, Alps, Himalayas and Rockies.

This constant swinging between cold and warm climatic regimes had a great

The annual temperature would fall only by a few degrees Celsius, but this was enough to spread kilometre-thick ice sheets across the globe

effect on the animals and plants of the world. This can be seen most clearly in Europe, Asia and America. Prior to the ice ages, the animal communities of the northern mid-latitudes were a rich and varied mixture of large herds of grazing animals, such as horse and deer, with many fleet-footed predators and scavengers, including the big cats, dogs and wolves. In amongst them were giant herbivores such as the elephants, rhinos and hippos.

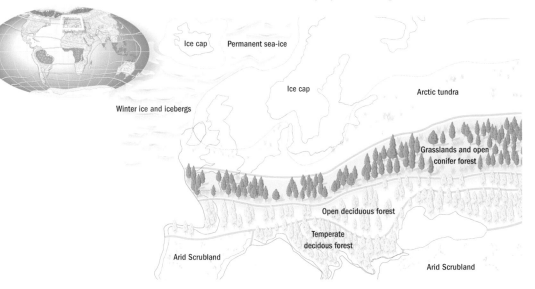

Ice cap Permanent sea-ice

Winter ice and icebergs

Ice cap

Arctic tundra

Grasslands and open conifer forest

Open deciduous forest

Temperate decidous forest

Arid Scrubland

Arid Scrubland

Devil in the detail
By 30,000 years ago, the configuration of the continents was almost identical to today. However, it was the middle of an ice age and all the water locked up in the ice sheets meant that sea levels were lower. A closer look at northern Europe reveals

how different this world was: permanent ice covered where St Petersburg, Oslo and London will be built, Arctic tundra grew over the Netherlands, neither the North Sea nor the English Channel existed, and icebergs floated off the coast of Ireland.

During the first ice ages most of these animals were driven further south in search of warmer weather and food, but in time many came to adapt themselves to the cold so that they could exploit the under-utilized food supplies that existed in front of the ice sheets. Many animals evolved a thick fur coat and a layer of fat to help them through the colder weather. This was certainly the case for the woolly mammoth and rhino, but the same was true for many small carnivores such as foxes, and for rabbits, cats, horses and bison. Animals also began to take advantage of the great difference in temperature between the seasons, moving north during the summer and back south again in winter. Thus it was that an entirely new ecosystem evolved, in which herds of deer, horses and mammoths moved backwards and forwards across a patchily wooded landscape, followed by predators. Eventually these animals were also to be joined by the primates *Homo erectus*, *Homo neanderthalensis* and *Homo sapiens*.

The effect of the ice ages was not confined to the extreme northern and southern parts of the globe. Each time the ice caps grew they sucked valuable heat and moisture from the atmosphere and oceans. Rain-dependent forests would shrink back towards river basins and coastlines while the deserts expanded.

As time progressed, so the ice ages became more severe and lasted for greater lengths of time. From around 300,000 years ago we start to see many species of once-common mammals becoming extinct. Although we are currently in a warm and relatively stable interglacial period, the Earth is still in the grip of the ice-age cycles, which means that our descendants may one day have to contend with the threat of the expanding ice caps.

Now you see him (LEFT) Like many polar animals, the arctic fox, here in his summer coat, turns completely white during winter.

Stubborn breeder (RIGHT) Bison are typical of the type of large mammals that do not migrate in winter. In the last ice age, woolly rhino probably did the same.

Woolly mammoth
The defining icon of the ice age, these magnificent creatures were hugely successful and the dominant herbivore across a huge swathe of the northern hemisphere grasslands. There were several types, but the 'woolly' variety (*Mammuthus primigenius*) was hairier and slightly smaller than its southern cousins — such as the Columbian mammoth mentioned in Chapter 3.
EVIDENCE: The woolly mammoth is known from bones and frozen carcasses from Ireland, across Europe and Russia, to the east coast of North America. The best preserved bodies have been found in Siberia.
SIZE: Males 3 metres (10 feet) tall, females 2.7 metres (9 feet) tall.
DIET: Grasses and sedges with some browsed twigs.
TIME: 135,000—11,000 years ago.

Rising up over the ridge comes the familiar bulk of a mammoth, her dense summer coat back lit by the failing sun. It is an old matriarch and she is leading a small herd of eight younger animals. On seeing the humans she raises her huge twisted tusks in threat and walks straight towards them. For a brief moment the humans weigh up the situation and consider trying to drag the carcass with them, but it is too heavy and on these open steppes everything eventually gives way to the mammoths. The human group scatters as the matriarch makes it clear she is not going to tolerate them anywhere near her herd. Although humans are rarely a threat to mammoths, the reason for her concern becomes clear as the rest of the herd appear over the hill. Ambling beneath his mother's shaggy flanks is a small calf and he would be vulnerable to the sophisticated hunting techniques humans often use to separate a youngster from its mother. This evening, however, the humans decide they have enough meat and, in the gathering gloom, they melt away into the landscape.

Moving past the carcass, the herd resume the important activity of feeding. During the summer, mammoths will sometimes feed all day and most of the night. A full-grown woolly mammoth weighs about 6–7 tonnes and needs about 180 kilograms (400 pounds) of food a day. Although it will eat just about any plant, including the leaves and bark of trees, grass makes up the majority of its diet. To watch a mammoth at work grazing is to watch a true specialist. The tip of its trunk can either pluck individual tasty morsels such as flowers or wrap round and rip up huge clumps of grass. The trunk then feeds a mouth containing gigantic grinding molars that smash up the toughest steppe vegetation and sends it on down to the mammoth's fermentation vat of a stomach. As the herd concentrates on their grazing only the youngster seems disinterested. He still gets most of his nutrition from his mother's milk and so has more time on his hands. Time for play, but also time to get into trouble.

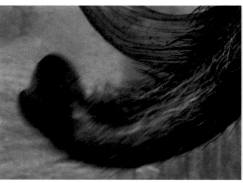

The mammoth's trunk is perfect for harvesting grass. The animal either wraps the trunk round large tussocks and uproots them, or its prehensile tip can pluck individual plants.

Big mummy

Each mammoth herd is a matriarchy led by an old female. Her size and power means she has nothing to fear from the human hunting party behind.

227

At the bottom of the valley is a small lake surrounded by particularly lush vegetation. Gradually the herd's grazing takes it nearer and nearer the lake's swampy shores. Suddenly the baby, who has been wandering ahead of his mother, slips into deep mud. He honks in alarm as his small limbs become trapped in the thick cold silt. Within seconds his mother, aunt and elder cousin are there to help him. As they strive to drag him out they also sink into the mud. However, it comes up only to their knees and soon a very dirty and chastened young mammoth is restored to his mother.

As night progresses, a cold wind arrives from the north. There are still several weeks of summer left, but the icy breeze is a timely reminder of the what is to come

The herd are a very close-knit group, which is not surprising since they are all related. The matriarch is about 40 years old and is accompanied by her 30-year-old sister – it is the latter's youngster they have just saved from the mud. The herd also contains the matriarch's three daughters, two of them are mature females, while the other is only four years old. There is only one male in the herd, other than the baby, and he is now a young adolescent. He will soon be ready to leave and, like all bull mammoths, he will live a solitary life seeking out receptive females among other herds.

As night progresses, a cold wind arrives from the north. There are still several weeks of summer left, but the icy breeze is a timely reminder of what is to come. In the distance the fires of a group of humans are visible against the jet-black landscape and the smell of burning mammoth bones is in the air. The shriek of a horse being attacked by hyaenas drifts through the darkness but none of this poses any threat to the giant mammoths – they calmly carry on feeding.

Protected for life
A female mammoth will stay within the herd for their entire lives — which sometimes can be almost 50 years.

September It is the megaloceros rutting season and already it is bitterly cold. Overnight the first fall of powdery snow has filled the gullies – this will not melt for five months. The grasses have turned brown and the dwarf birch have shed their leaves. In just over a month the landscape has transformed. Many of the summer visitors have left and herds of bison and reindeer have been on the move all day. The mammoth herds will soon join them, but for now they are still scraping the last out of their summer grazing grounds. The matriarch uses her tusks to sweep away a patch of the light snow and starts tearing up thick wads of moss. Since August the mammoths' appearance has changed somewhat with the growth of their winter coat. It is darker and longer, turning them their distinctive chocolate brown colour and giving them a hairy 'skirt' of guard hairs. As the cold wind catches and blows this around, their soft pale underwool is visible below.

On a barren hillside nearby a harem of megaloceros wait for two gigantic males to sort out who will mate with them. Both are in their prime and, as they issue their series of bellowing challenges, clouds of vapour drift up past their magnificent antlers. Slowly they size each other up while they move higher and higher up the side of a hill, each trying to gain an advantage over the other. Unfortunately both are about the same size and age with matching 3-metre- (10-feet) wide antlers. Neither is going to give way without a fight.

As they approach the ridge one male rears up and brings his antlers crashing down on the second. His opponent is ready for this and makes sure their antlers match and lock. Now begins a fearsome trial of strength. The pair wheel round again and again as each animal tries to use the slope to give himself an advantage. Their grunts and the clatter of their antlers echo round the valley. Unfortunately for the megaloceros, the mammoths are not the only witnesses to this sexual contest. In a dense stand of larch a hunting group of humans have their own interest in the fight.

Megaloceros

Megaloceros is often called the 'Irish elk', although it was found all across Europe and is technically a deer rather than an elk. A bizarre early theory was that its huge antlers were its downfall, because they grew so large that the animals could no longer lift their heads. It is now thought there must have been a significant sexual advantage for males with large antlers, hence some grew to over 3 metres (10 feet) across.

EVIDENCE: *Megaloceros* fossils are found in large numbers, especially in the peat bogs of Ireland. Most of them are males suffering from malnutrition, presumably after the autumn rutting season. They are also seen in cave paintings, which indicate their colour patterns.

SIZE: 2 metres (6 feet 6 inches) at the shoulder.

DIET: Grass and browsed vegetation from the edges of woodlands.

TIME: 400,000–9500 years ago.

Eventually the males break with a clear winner and the exhausted loser is driven away from the harem. It happens that he was the incumbent male and had probably already had to fight three or four times before this season to defend his harem. Now he stands by the larch, breathing heavily, covered in cuts and drained by his ordeal. This is what the humans were waiting for. With their massive antlers and standing over 2 metres (6.5 feet) at the shoulders, megaloceros are fearsome adversaries, so humans rarely attack mature animals. But things are different at this time of year. Food is scarce and, like all the other creatures here, the humans need to feed up before moving south. Also the rut has a devastating effect on the strength of male megaloceros, making them easier prey.

Three humans, covered in animal skins and brandishing spears, approach the defeated male from the open, driving him towards the larch. He stops short of the trees and prepares to charge, but the humans start to throw stones to keep him at bay. Then a spear cuts the megaloceros's shoulder. He moves along the clump of larch, but as he does so another human appears out of the trees. Panicked, the male turns towards the wood and his antlers become tangled in the branches. The humans rush him. He catches one with his antlers, but the fight is lost. The hunters use their spears ruthlessly, first incapacitating and then killing the male.

Through the morning the wind has been gradually growing stronger and, as the humans huddle round their kill, the mammoth matriarch decides it is time to leave. With a weather system moving off towards the east, even colder temperatures are being dragged down from the north – this is the matriarch's cue to head south. Mammoths are not truly migratory like reindeer, but they do not remain on these exposed open plains during the ice-age winter. To the south lie more sheltered valleys and they will overwinter there. As the herd move off, a pack of wolves appear to the south. They have smelt the megaloceros kill and hope to scavenge their share.

Stag at bay

The male megaloceros has huge antlers 3 metres (10 feet) across but, working as a team, human hunting parties have worked out how to corner and kill one of these majestic beasts.

Heading for pastures new
Through blizzards and temperatures of –20°C, the herd head for winter grazing in the sheltered valleys to the south. The snow settled on their backs and heads shows how well-insulated they are.

October The open steppes are deserted, the mammoth-bone huts built by humans are abandoned and the only visible animals are the few musk oxen scraping for moss beneath the snow. The mammoth herds are all drifting south, each led by a matriarch who can remember the route. Our herd are already well on their way – their leader has made this journey over 40 times and knows which valleys are best to winter in. One of the younger females is pregnant and, since mammoth pregnancies last two years, this is the third time she has had to travel while carrying. However, her trial will not be as bad as that of the youngster. He was born only in the late spring and this is the first time he has had to move so far or face such consistently low temperatures. His mother sticks close by him, but their pace is slower than the others and they frequently fall behind.

After several kilometres a heavy blizzard blows in from the west and the mother has to stop and shelter her baby. By the time it clears they have become separated from the herd. She calls out, but the rest are too far away – it is now up to her alone to lead the youngster to safety. The mother calls again and this time she gets a response – but not, unfortunately, from a mammoth. Through the last flurries of the receding blizzard a slight movement on a ridge ahead betrays the presence of a predator. The mother cannot see it, but she can smell it – a lion. He is the most powerful predator here and much larger than his African counterparts. With fur-covered feet and a pale coat the lion moves like a ghost over the snowy hills. He is shadowing the mammoths, looking for a chance to grab the baby. At one point he stalks too close and the mother instantly attacks. He backs off – despite his size and power he will not attack unless the

> Our herd are already well on their way – their leader has made this journey over 40 times and knows which valleys are best to winter in

233

European (Cave) lion
Lions have been around in Africa for at least 3.5 million years, but they first appeared in Europe 900,000 years ago, and since that time became reasonably common. The European lions are slightly larger than their African cousins, which probably helped them hunt some of the larger herbivores on the great European plains, such as bison. Cave paintings of European lions suggest they had no mane or tuft at the end of the tail, although it could be that the paintings are of females.
EVIDENCE: Common in Europe, with especially large numbers being found at Geilenreuth in Germany and Wierzchowskiej Gornej in Poland.
SIZE: About 1.5m at the shoulder.
DIET: Horses, deer and bison.
TIME: 900,000—10,000 years ago.

youngster is separated from his giant protector. The mother stops calling and moves off warily.

Ahead the herd have other concerns. The adolescent male has fallen through some ice and become trapped in freezing cold water. The rest of the herd have gathered round, but are powerless to help without risking the same fate. Beneath the thin blanket of snow this countryside is full of ponds, lakes and streams that freeze over in the winter. Many, however, cannot support the weight of a mature mammoth and this miserable fate is all too common among these gentle giants. The young male is submerged up to his shoulders and the mixture of smashed ice, water and mud round him offers nothing to help him clamber out. His coat is soaked, adding to his weight and his troubles. The matriarch reaches out with her trunk, apparently more in reassurance than in an attempt to pull him out. The scene is witnessed by a group of humans, but they will not attempt to scavenge the dying mammoth. The rest of the herd may well stand by the corpse for days, protecting it, and the humans cannot afford to wait in this exposed position for that long. As they disappear, the young mammoth's life slowly ebbs away.

This delay means the mother and her baby unwittingly overtake the rest of their herd. As they approach the southern uplands and valleys, the changing geography forces many migrating animals together. This is perhaps the only time of the year when it is possible to appreciate the wealth of life that feeds on the steppes. The mother joins the procession, her baby still stumbling along at her side. With all these other herds around, the youngster will be safe from the lion. Besides, it would seem that the predator has found other prey. In woods overlooking the escarpment the lion watches the mammoth, his white coat spattered in red. He is standing over a bundle of fur which contains a human – a much easier prey for a predator of his size.

No competition
A cave lion sporting his white winter coat attempts to stalk a baby mammoth; but its mother is aware of the danger and the lion has no chance of reaching the youngster while she is in attendance.

Old favourite
Mammoths have been popular in palaentological exhibitions since the Victorian era, this one appeared in 1860 in the St Petersburg Museum.

All skin and bone
Despite being thousands of years old, mammoth meat can be fresh enough to eat. Luckily this baby was not found by scavengers first.

Ice giants

Around the Arctic Circle, particularly in Siberia, the ground is permanently frozen, down to a depth of 500 metres (1600 feet). In the brief Arctic summers since the last ice age, only the top 1.5 metres (5 feet) or so has ever thawed out. Below that is nature's deep freeze. Every spring, the great Siberian rivers swell with meltwater, and erode their banks. It is usually along these banks that the bodies of animals which have died and been frozen for tens of thousands of years are found. Bison, woolly rhinos and mammoths are all regularly discovered, but this does not necessarily mean that a carcass will be available to scientists. It has been estimated that hundreds or possibly

thousands of carcasses have been uncovered over the years. In the vastness of Siberia many of these are never discovered by humans and the fresh meat ends up as food for hungry carnivores. Even if local people do find one they may not report it. In some areas local folklore maintains that the discovery of a mammoth will bring death to the family of those who uncover it. Others have learned that the interest generated by such a discovery can be disruptive to their lives: an expedition in 1799 to excavate a mammoth carcass enslaved the local tribe and forced them to dig the body out of the solid, frozen earth. Even present-day Siberian geologists claim that many corpses are destroyed every year by miners who fear that the arrival of scientists will bring a halt to their mining activities.

However, those that do reach the scientists have given us huge amounts of information. A close analysis of the soil around the body and the stomach contents can give clues about the plants which grew at the time, but, perhaps most excitingly, the frozen conditions can preserve the flesh of the animal well enough for its DNA to survive. This has raised the possibility of cloning extinct animals.

Bare bones (LEFT)
The mammoth skeleton does not show the familiar sloping back which is depicted in cave paintings.

Giant graveyard (BELOW)
At Hot Springs in South Dakota, more than 47 mammoth skeletons have been found, leading to theories that this was some kind of boggy trap.

So far, mammoth DNA has been extracted successfully from Siberian carcasses, and has told us that they were closely related to all the living elephant species. However, the amount of DNA we have at the moment is far too small to be able to clone a mammoth.

The word mammoth seems to have come from a Siberian dialect, meaning 'earth mole', as many locals believed that these were living creatures which burrowed underground and died if they ever came into contact with the light – explaining why they were never seen alive. The European woolly mammoth, *Mammuthus primigenius*, is the best-known species, not only because about a dozen frozen carcasses have been found, but because it features in the art of modern humans, who lived

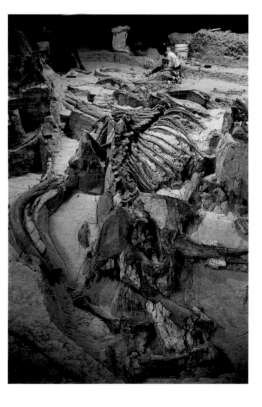

alongside them in Europe for tens of thousands of years. One of the most obvious features of the paintings is the mammoth's sloping back – the hind legs look much shorter than the front legs. Looking at the skeletons we have, though, the hind and front legs are almost the same length. The hump behind the head shown in the art must have been made up of fat, muscle or hair, but unfortunately no adult mammoth has been preserved well enough to tell us which.

The art and frozen carcasses also give us a lot of information about the mammoths' hair. With just the skeletons we might never have known that woolly mammoths were woolly at all.

One site in South Dakota, USA, gives us a surprising insight. Here was a mammoth trap – a thermally heated pond at the bottom of a steep-sided hole. Around the pond, lush vegetation would have grown at all times of year, and this obviously attracted animals which could then not escape back up the sides of the pit. The mammoths, though, are almost all adolescent males. Among modern elephants, the females stick together and it is the lone males that are most likely to explore a trap like this pit and be on their own should they get stuck.

Neanderthal

The first Neanderthal remains were found in the Neander valley in Germany in 1856. Nearly ten years later a detailed study of the bones revealed that they were different from those of modern humans, and they were given the species name *Homo neanderthalensis*.

EVIDENCE: Neanderthal remains have been found in a broad band from the Middle East across to Britain and down to the northern edge of the Mediterranean. These include bones, campsites and tools, but as far as we know there are no artistic representations of them.

SIZE: Males 1.7 metres (5 feet 6 inches) tall, females 1.6 metres (5 feet 3 inches).

DIET: Almost exclusively meat.

TIME: 300,000—28,000 years ago.

November In the more rugged country to the south of the steppe, the vegetation changes. There are more forests of birch, alder and willow, giving the animals that live here more shelter and a wider range of food. This suits creatures such as the Neanderthals, another type of human who are better adapted to endure the cold and who stay here all year round. Living in small groups, they also use furs to protect themselves from the colder weather, but they are shorter and stockier than their cousins. However, although they evolved to thrive in these conditions, Their population is in decline and they now only survive in small pockets. In fact, humans as a group are not as varied as they once were: these two species may be the only ones left.

Every winter the mammoths come off the steppe and disperse into these valleys, surviving on a diet of bark, evergreen twigs and what grass and herbs they can find amongst the snow. Generally they stick to the more open areas since they are not forest animals. In one such valley the matriarch arrives with her herd. It has been a bad journey – she has lost one nephew and her sister and other nephew are still missing. The herd stop near a cliff that contains Neanderthal caves and the matriarch pushes over a willow so that they can all eat the few leaves that still cling to its upper branches. Smoke from the Neanderthals' fires curls up in front of the caves as the humans watch the mammoth warily – these are dangerous neighbours. One of the group has been away collecting firewood and on his return is forced to take a long detour to avoid the herd. However, this brings him face to face with an even more unpredictable foe. On clearing a group of alder to the left of the herd he stumbles into a clearing already occupied by a woolly rhino. Like the lions these northern rhinos are slightly larger than their African cousins. They have a thick winter coat and extraordinarily long horns, sometimes up to 2 metres (6.5 feet) long. Most of the time these are used for clearing snow, but they also double as

Nearest and dearest

The extinction of the Neanderthals is an unsolved mystery in the story of human evolution. Although it is traditionally believed that they were either killed by our ancestors, *Homo sapiens,* or died out because of the effects of the last ice age, many people also think they could have disappeared because they interbred with modern humans and that over several dozen generations all the Neanderthal traits disappeared.

Until recently there was no accurate means of judging whether Neanderthals and modern humans ever met and interbred, but recent advances in the science of genetics have gone some way to solving this conundrum.

As all our genes are inherited from our forebears, if one or more of our ancient relatives was born of mixed Neanderthal and modern human parentage, there should still be remnants of Neanderthal DNA in our genes. Unfortunately, until recently nobody knew what Neanderthal DNA looked like and so had no idea whether or not it was present in today's modern humans.

All this changed in the late 1990s when DNA was extracted from several Neanderthal bones and compared with human DNA. The results were negative and

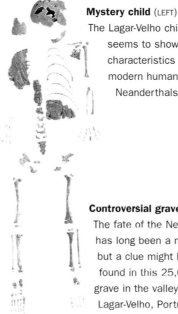

Mystery child (LEFT)
The Lagar-Velho child's skeleton seems to show characteristics of both modern humans and Neanderthals.

Controversial grave (RIGHT)
The fate of the Neanderthals has long been a mystery, but a clue might have been found in this 25,000-year-old grave in the valley of the Lagar-Velho, Portugal.

it looked as though the Neanderthals and modern humans kept themselves to themselves after all. However, a chance discovery in Portugal in 1998 complicated the issue. Workmen bulldozing a cliff in the

If one or more of our ancient relatives was born of mixed Neanderthal and modern human parentage, there should still be remnants of Neanderthal DNA in our genes

valley of Lagar-Velho found the skeleton of a small child who had been ritually buried about 25,000 years ago. When the skeleton was examined it seemed to have the robust bones of a Neanderthal but the facial structure of a modern human. This led to a suggestion that the child could have been born to mixed Neanderthal and modern human parents. However, the skull of the skeleton is mostly missing which makes it difficult to be certain whether the child had some Neanderthal characteristics or was simply a robust human. Scientists have reached a deadlock until further evidence can be found.

Woolly rhino
The horns of the woolly rhino (*Coelodonta antiquitatis*) were often found in Russia during the nineteenth century, but because they are so strange-looking, many people believed that they were the claws of giant birds. Frozen carcasses of woolly rhinos were occasionally found in Siberia, although often without their horns or hair, but eventually it was realized that the two belonged together.

EVIDENCE: Rhino remains have been found all across Europe, although they apparently did not reach Ireland or North America. Again the best-preserved carcasses are found in Siberia. They are also depicted in cave paintings, some of which suggest they may have had a band of darker fur around their middles.

SIZE: 2.2 metres (7 feet) at the shoulder.
DIET: Grass.
TIME: 500,000–10,000 years ago.

fearsome weapons. To make matters worse, like all rhinos, woollies are short-sighted and easily-startled.

The rhino smells the Neanderthal immediately and snorts aggressively. The human stops and starts very slowly to retrace his steps. He knows how dangerous the rhino can be, since both animals stay in the same place all year round. But this also means the rhino knows the scent of Neanderthal and he recognizes a carnivore when he smells one. The Neanderthal approaches the trees, then turns to run for his caves. The rhino sees this movement and, probably thinking that he is being attacked, he charges. The rhino is fast and the human is slowed by his furs. Before he can reach the denser trees the rhino catches him a glancing blow with his horn, sending him reeling against a birch stump. The whole episode hardly takes a second and, after the Neanderthal has lain motionless for a few moments, the rhino snorts and wanders off. However, the rhino weighs well over 2 tonnes and the Neanderthal only about 70 kilograms (150 pounds). The blow has shattered his hip and leg. With a whole winter ahead of him he will survive only if his group manage to help him through. Even so, his hunting days are definitely over.

Later that day, the mammoths move away from the caves and spend the night near a large lake that has yet to freeze. The next morning a mist hangs over the water, but the day is still and bright. The herd's casual feeding and drinking is transformed by a low call and a series of short, high-pitched honks. Round the far shore come the missing mother and her baby to rejoin their herd. The same unfailing memory that allows the matriarch to lead them every year to the best valleys has served her sister well and she has drastically improved the chances of her little one surviving the winter by tracking down his aunt. They greet with the usual grappling of trunks and clattering of tusks. From the herd's perspective the journey south now seems not to have been too bad.

The enormously long horns of the woolly rhino are very useful for self defence, but in practice the rhino uses them much more frequently for clearing snow so it can find winter food. To help them in their search, the front horn is shaped like a blade.

Dangerous neighbour

A Neanderthal desperately defends himself against an approaching woolly rhino; however, his only real hope is that the huge short-tempered beast just loses interest.

March The winter is long and relentless. Across northern Europe temperatures struggle to get above freezing, with an average temperature of –7° Celsius (19.4° F). The eventual approach of spring is signalled by a small rise in average temperature which is enough to start the melt. Across the landscape rivers swell with icy water and along their banks the earliest flowers and herbs break through the slush.

During the winter the mammoth herd have not moved far. The valley in which they arrived four months ago has been big enough to support them, even though numerous trees have suffered from their destructive eating habits. There is also a new addition to the herd. The pregnant mammoth has given birth early and a small fluffy baby female is sticking very close to her side. With luck she now faces many decades with the same companions, as she will spend her whole life in the herd. As these huge, lumbering creatures move about, they show remarkable delicacy when dealing with the infant and, as with all mammoth herds, her aunts and nieces seem almost as concerned about her welfare as her mother.

As more and more fresh new grazing appears for the herd, the pressure on the herd to find food eases. However, things are not as rosy as they might seem. The sudden flush in new growth is rich in certain minerals, but deficient in others. Not only that, but many herbs carry a lot of toxins at this time of year. All this means that the spring growth can play havoc with the normally cast-iron digestive system of the mammoths. Again it is the experience of the matriarch and the other older females that pays off for the herd. Through the slowly emerging meadows they lead the herd out of the valley to an area of muddy swamp. Here the matriarch sets the example by starting to eat mud. Bizarre though this may seem, the clay is useful for neutralizing the toxins and it contains many of the vital minerals that the new growth is missing. Soon the other herd members join in, scraping up lumps of clay with their tusks and eating them.

Spring flush
Once the snow melts the herd can start feeding again in earnest. Soon the beasts are cropping almost 200 kilograms of vegetation a day.

The only one who refuses to take his vitamins is the yearling. With the help of his mother's milk he has survived winter well and he shows no inclination to eat mud. Instead, he finds a much more enjoyable use for the swamp – rolling in it. Soon his dense fur is caked in it and he ambles between the adults, sharing bits with them. Later, as the mud dries, lumps fall off and with it patches of longer hair. The yearling is beginning to moult. It is time to head north.

Mixed company (OVERLEAF)
With all the new spring growth, many animals have problems balancing the minerals in their diet. One solution is to eat mud – which also helps neutralize toxins.

April It is late evening when the herd approaches the escarpment. Six months ago hundreds of herds of mammoths passed through here on their way south and now their northward journey has brought them back. There is less snow than there was in the autumn, and the Neanderthals who live beneath the escarpment are much busier then they were before. Along its length they are carrying wood and constructing small piles next to the mammoths' route.

As night falls the Neanderthals light the wood piles, pick up brands and start to make fake runs at the mammoths which are still moving along the escarpment. The herd is caught in the centre of this attack and it is a very dangerous place to be. The Neanderthals' aim is to panic and confuse the mammoth so that they can drive some over the cliff edge. They get this opportunity only once a year, but it provides them with a bonanza. Gradually they push closer and closer. The matriarch trumpets in alarm and the agitation of the herds around her adds to her distress. The fire makes her reluctant to charge, but eventually one Neanderthal gets too

Murder in mind

A Neanderthal collects wood for a fire. Over the years they have learnt to use fire to hunt prey that is too large and powerful to be killed by hand.

End of the line
The herd matriarch is eventually driven to the edge of the cliff by Neanderthals wielding fiery brands. Every year these predators try to kill mammoths in this way.

close. The huge mammoth swings her tusks, knocking him and the brand away. He is soon trampled underfoot as the rest of the herd retreat from his companions.

Mammoth herds stay together and, although many escape the Neanderthals, almost all our herd becomes trapped against the cliff edge – all except the baby mammoth, who has had trouble keeping pace. She has become isolated away from the cliff. On realizing this her mother charges through the advancing Neanderthals to rejoin her infant. This breaks the ring of fire and scatters their attackers. The herd head for the gap, but one is caught behind – the matriarch. Now almost berserk with fear, she swings her tusks at the Neanderthals. Eventually she steps back too far and stumbles off the cliff. It is a fall of less than 15 metres (50 feet), but it is enough to kill her.

The next morning is cold and wet; a thick fog hangs around the base of the escarpment as the Neanderthals set about their grisly task of stripping the huge carcass with their flint tools. In fact three mammoths fell to their deaths the night before, providing the Neanderthals with more meat than they can possible handle. It is unusual for predators to kill so much more than they need, but it is a feature of this kind of hunting. In some years, it can have a severe effect on the mammoth herds. As the humans work, wolves are already gathering nearby. The Neanderthals take as much hide as they can and the choice cuts of meat, such as the tongue.

During the night the mammoth herd regroup and then wait for the return of the matriarch. They wait for a further two days on the escarpment before the old matriarch's sister leads them away and once again starts the move to the north.

Three mammoths fell to their deaths the night before, providing the Neanderthals with more meat than they can possible handle

Killer apes

Both Neanderthals and modern humans were, by most animal standards, extremely inventive hunters. Although we automatically think that the natural prey of Stone-Age humans would be woolly mammoths and rhinos, these animals would have presented a considerable danger because of their size. Instead we mostly find the bones of more manageable animals such as deer, horses, rabbits and foxes.

Up to about 35,000 years ago, both species hunted in much the same manner, using sticks and spears. After this time differences in hunting techniques begin to emerge. The technology of the Neanderthals, while functional, was fairly basic. Their spears were simply sharpened sticks which would have been thrust into their prey at close range. By contrast the modern humans had built spears with sharpened points of antler or flint, which could be launched from quite a distance away. By about 30,000 years ago modern humans were beginning to use advanced technology to their advantage. There is evidence that they may have made nets to catch rabbits or fish and that they were developing special launching systems for their spears that could propel them accurately over dozens of metres. The Neanderthals did not show similar

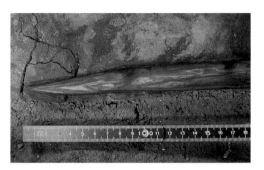

Murder weapon
This 400,000-year-old spear was found embedded in horse bones at a site in Germany. It is a rare find, not only because it is direct evidence of hunting, but also because it is so old.

Unnatural enemies
Although the evidence suggests that humans rarely tackled prey as large as elephants, as this cave painting from Africa shows, it must have happened.

innovations until only a thousand or so years before their extinction.

However, possibly the greatest innovation in 'mass' hunting came from the Neanderthals. On the Channel Island of Jersey there is a cave at the bottom of

The animals were probably chased over the edge of the cliff by the Neanderthals at minimum risk to themselves

a steep cliff in which the bones of many woolly mammoths and rhinos were found next to Neanderthal tools. They had clearly been killed at the site and then carefully stripped of meat and stacked – but how could so many large animals have been killed in one go by only a small tribe of Neanderthals? The answer came from the archaeologist Kate Scott. She examined the bones and suggested that the animals were probably chased over the edge of the cliff by the Neanderthals, at minimum risk to themselves. The injured or dead animals could then have been eaten at leisure.

June It is the height of summer on the steppe. Humans once again occupy their bone huts and the herds have returned to graze on the deep, lush grass. The air is full of midges. For the mammoth, now in their shorter summer coats, these insects are an irritation. Occasionally they tear up bunches of grass just to swish them away, but their main defence is the long hairy tail that works constantly to disperse the swarms. The baby mammoth is particularly vulnerable and when she is not feeding she stands behind her mother, taking advantage of the big fly swat above her. She has survived the journey north well, although from the look of a torn and damaged ear she only just escaped the attentions of some predators. The most likely culprits are hyaenas, which frequently try to separate very young mammoths from their parents at night. In this case the herd were obviously up to the challenge.

Despite the midges the herd are in good condition. The new matriarch is established in her position and one of the younger females has come into season. This has attracted the attention of two males, both even larger than the matriarch, with huge curling tusks. Their presence is making the herd nervous, because the yearling and the baby could be injured as these huge males compete for the female. After they have sized each other up, amid much waggling of ears and shaking of heads, the slightly older male charges. With a sickening thump and clatter the two rivals lock tusks and use their muscular trunks to tussle for an advantage. Both weigh over 7 tonnes and are risking severe injury in the fight. It has been known for the participants to become so locked together and exhausted that they die, unable to separate themselves even to feed. However, this is what they have been preparing for ever since they left their mothers' herd and if they fail to mate successfully then, in an evolutionary sense, their lives have been a failure.

The fight lasts about an hour before the older animal asserts his dominance and the younger one is forced into retreat. In a heightened

Tusk force
Two male mammoths celebrate their arrival in the summer pastures by starting a fight. The struggle for dominance and the right to mate is a constant feature of their lives.

Afterword Within a few thousands years the ice age did come to a close. The ice sheets started to retreat to their present positions. Forests once again flourished across the higher latitudes of the northern hemisphere and, in the tropics, the rainforests replaced drier grasslands. However, the latest research suggests that the shift to the current warmer interglacial period, with all its climactic and environmental changes, was very fast, lasting perhaps as little as a few decades. This must have put enormous pressure on all the plants and animals but especially the highly specialized, larger creatures. Gradually, one by one, the giants of the ice age died out. Even the mighty woolly mammoth was driven to extinction, while the last pitiful population of pygmy mammoths clung on until 10,000 years ago on an island off eastern Siberia.

Should anyone start to feel complacent about our future it is worth remembering that, at least theoretically, another ice age is due

As for our human ancestors – in the ice age we were just another animal surviving in a grim world. However, our inventive use of tools was unique and seems to have helped us as the Earth warmed. Generation after generation then built on its experience and gradually improved our ability to control our environment and escape the slavery of day-to-day survival. This set us on a course that would eventually create the 'unnatural' creatures we are today. But should anyone start to feel complacent about our future, it is worth remembering that, at least theoretically, another ice age is due. If it were to arrive over a couple of decades, the ice sheets could cover everything north of London and the world's agriculture would be turned on its head. Would we be able to adapt? We too are a highly specialized creature and, when all is said and done, just another large mammal.

Passing of an era (OVERLEAF)
As temperatures drop for the winter the mammoths are on the move, but their highly-specialized lifestyle makes them vulnerable to climatic change. In only a few thousand years the vast herds of mammoth will completely disappear from the Earth.

Source material

Chapter 1

The Messel oil shales, near Frankfurt, Germany provided much of the information for this chapter. Excellent specimens of *Leptictidium*, *Propalaeotherium* and *Godinotia* have all been recovered from the Messel (pages 56–7). Some of these specimens have preserved hair and even stomach contents. Many other types of animal, and plant life from this time are also preserved in the shales, which give us a very accurate picture of this ancient environment. *Gastornis* is only known in the Messel from the imprint of one isolated bone. However, *Gastornis* fossils are more common in the nearby Geiseltal shales (which are of similar age and environment to the Messel) and near-complete skeletons are found in North America. *Ambulocetus* is not known from the Messel at all but in fact comes from Pakistan; the chemistry of its teeth shows that it lived in both brackish and fresh water. Both the Messel and Geiseltal sites were surrounded by the Tethys Sea at that time.

Chapter 2

The brontothere seen in this chapter is based on *Embolotherium*, a large animal whose remains have been found chiefly in Mongolia. *Andrewsarchus* is only known from one gigantic skull, also found in Mongolia. However, complete skeletons of many of its close relatives, called mesonychians, have been preserved, which is how we know what *Andrewsarchus'* body looked like. *Basilosaurus* and *Dorudon* skeletons are known from America, Europe and Asia but most of our information was gleaned from the Egyptian Fayum formation rocks near Cairo (pages 86–7). The skeletons of *Apidium* and *Moeritherium* have also been found in the Fayum rocks, along with fossilized mangrove trees, sea grass and other plants and animals – all of which indicate a coastal/estuarine setting. The Fayum rocks were laid down across the boundary between the Eocene and Oligocene epochs, when vast environmental changes caused a moderate mass extinction event on Earth, especially among marine life.

Chapter 3

The animals and plants portrayed in this chapter all come from the Hsanda Gol Formation (page 131) of Mongolia. Some animals, such as the indricothere, have been found almost in their entiret. Others, such as *Hyaenodon*, chalicothere and bear-dog are only known from disarticulated remains. Fortunately, some of the Hsanda Gol species we wanted to portray are also found in North America, where many complete skeletons have been found in areas such as Agate Springs National Monument, Nebraska. Much of our behavioural evidence, such as the collapsed bear-dog burrows, also came from fossils found in Agate Springs. Our chalicothere is based on material that was mostly recovered from Germany. The Hsanda Gol rocks are also very poor in plant fossils, but equivalent rocks with plant fossils have been found just to the north in southern China. Our botanical and climatic information was taken from there.

Chapter 4

The central characters of this chapter are the early hominid *Australopithecus afarensis* whose fossil remains have been found in Ethiopia, Tanzania and Kenya. Reasonably complete skeletons like that of 'Lucy', from Hadar in Ethiopia (pages 176–7), were used to recreate *Australopithecus afarensis* and pathological evidence from their bones and teeth told us much about their diet, bipedal ability and general lifestyle. Specific behaviour, such as nesting, was taken from studies of living bonobos and chimpanzees. Both *Ancylotherium* and *Deinotherium* fossils have been found in association with fossil hominid sites, including Hadar, Laetoli, Lake Turkana and Olduvai Gorge. However, complete skeletons of both animals have only been found in Europe and it is upon these remains that our models are based. Much of the look and behaviour of *Dinofelis* we portrayed came from extensive work performed on cave deposits in South Africa where both *Australopithecus* and *Dinofelis* remains have been found together.

Bibliography

Chapter 5

Although many of the animals in this chapter roamed across South America, the majority of fossil and environmental information used came from a suite of rocks in Argentina called the Lujanian Formations; where the largest concentration of *Macrauchenia*, *Doedicurus* and *Megatherium* remains have been found. Carapaces of *Doedicurus* often bear the dents of mating fights and their biology is similar to that of living armadillos (although on a much bigger scale). Similarly, the dung and even hair and skin of *Megatherium* has been found in Chilean caves, and at Pehuen-Co, Argentina, there are rows of perfectly preserved footprints. The *Smilodon* species we used is endemic to the eastern side of South America, but Argentina has good fossil material too. In addition, we used the extensive studies performed on the dozens of *Smilodon* recovered from the La Brea tar pits, California. *Phorusrhacos* fossils are very rare and are more commonly found in the southern United States than South America. A recently recovered specimen from a Florida sinkhole suggests that this bird may have had clawed wings.

Chapter 6

The frozen mammoth and woolly rhino corpses of the sub-Arctic are ideal for reconstructing the look of these animals and provided us with dietary information. We also, for the first time, had eye witness evidence in the form of cave paintings. Observations of living elephants and rhinos revealed much behavioural information. Complete *Megaloceros* and cave lion skeletons have been found in many parts of Europe. There have been many thousands of Neanderthal and Cro-Magnon finds but we particularly focused our attention on ancient campsites found in Alsace, the Dordogne and Gibraltar. The capabilities and social behaviour of the humans were taken from detailed studies of these campsites and from observations of modern low-technology societies. Much of the migration information was taken from the study of Arctic tribal people's behaviour in relation to large prey such as reindeer. The La Cotte de St Brelade Neanderthal campsite in Jersey, the Channel Islands, was the basis for the mammoth hunt.

Behrensmeyer, A. K. *et al.*, *Terrestrial Ecosystems Through Time*, University of Chicago Press (1992)

Benton, M., *The Rise of the Mammals*, Eagle Editions (1998)

Benton, M., *Vertebrate Palaeontology*, Blackwell (2000)

Fleagle, J. G., *Primate Adaptation and Evolution*, Academic Press (1988)

Fortey, R., *Life – An Unauthorised Biography*, Flamingo (1998)

Gould, S. J., *The Book of Life*, W. W. Norton & Co.(2001)

Jones, S., Martin, R., Pilbeam, D. & Bunney, S., *The Cambridge Encyclopaedia of Human Evolution*, Cambridge University Press (1994)

Lister, A. & Bahn, P., *Mammoths*, Boxtree (1995)

McKie, R., *Apeman – The Story of Human Evolution*, BBC (2000)

MacDonald, D., *The Encyclopaedia of Mammals*, Equinox Ltd (1989)

MacDonald, D., *The Velvet Claw – A Natural History of the Carnivores*, BBC (1992)

Mellars, P., *The Neanderthal Legacy*, Princeton University Press (1996)

Norman, D., *Prehistoric Life*, Boxtree (1994)

Palmer, D., *The Marshall Illustrated Encyclopaedia of Dinosaurs and Prehistoric Animals*, Marshall Editions Ltd. (1999)

Palmer, D., *Atlas of the Prehistoric World*, Marshall Editions Ltd. (1999)

Prothero, D. R., *The Eocene-Oligocene Transition – Paradise Lost*, Columbia University Press (1994)

Schaal, S. & Ziegler, W., *Messel – An Insight into the History of Life and of the Earth*, Clarendon Press (1992)

Spinar, Z. V,. *Life before Man*, Thames and Hudson (1996)

Stringer, C. & Gamble, C., *In Search of the Neanderthals*, Thames & Hudson (1995)

Thewissen, J. G. M., *The Emergence of Whales*, Plenum Press (1998)

Turner, A. & Antón, M., *The Big Cats and their Fossil Relatives*, Columbia University Press (1997)

Zimmer, C., *At the Water's Edge – Macroevolution and the Transformation of Life*, Simon & Schuster (1998)

Index

Acknowledgements

Picture credits

In order to create something like this book I have had to rely on a huge team of highly-skilled people. I would like to thank everyone who was involved, many of whom I have had the honour to work with since the beginning of *Walking with Dinosaurs* four years ago. However, in particular, I am grateful to Mike Milne, who led Framestore's 3-D team and whose guidance and skills made these images possible, and Jasper James, who headed the BBC team that made the television series that accompanies this book. I am also very grateful to the location photographers who captured the backplates that are the starting point for all these pictures. They are Mike Pitts, Mark Duffy, Ernie Janes and, notably, Ian MacDonald, and also to Jez Harris and his talented team for all the models that appear in these pictures. A big thank you to the hundreds of skilled scientists on whose work this book is based, especially Dr Alex Freeman and Dr Paul Chambers who were the researchers on the television series and who helped in the writing of this book. Finally, thank you to my lovely wife Clare who put up with the late nights and kept my four little ones at bay long enough for me to write this.   TIM HAINES

I would like to thank my team of talented artists who helped me make these images better than I could have ever hoped. Firstly, Martin Macrae and my brother Jason Horley for producing some fantastic artwork for the animals' skin textures, and for seamlessly integrating the beasts into the backgrounds. Danny Geurtsen and Virginie Degorgue for their help in painting the animal's skins, David Hulin and Richard Ducker for posing and lighting the animals, Rob Farrar for lending a hand placing the beasts in scene. Many thanks also to Sarah Tosh, David Marsh and the team of digital modelers, John Veal, Oliver Cook, Jamie Isles, who put in so much hard work to meet those punishing deadlines. A big thanks also to Mike Milne and Sharon Reed for allowing me to take on the task in spite of my already busy schedule. Finally, I would like to thank my wife Aki for putting up with my obsession with all things prehistoric and for giving birth to our daughter, Emi, just as the pictures were finished – perfect timing!   DAREN HORLEY

BBC Worldwide would like to thank the following for providing photographs and for permission to reproduce copyright material. While every effort has been made to trace and acknowledge copyright holders, we would like to apologize should there have been any errors or omissions.

Page 26 (above) Oxford Scientific Films © Daniel J. Cox, (below) Robert Harding Picture Library; 27 (left) Bruce Coleman Collection © Alain Compost, (right) Ardea London © Ferrero-Labat; 30 © Spurlock Museum, Illinois; 37 (above) Robert Harding Picture Library, (below) Senckenberg, Messel Research Department; 44 (above) Ardea London, (below) Senckenberg, Messel Research Department; 56–7 Senckenberg, Messel Research Department; 58 Corbis Images; 64 Bruce Coleman Collection © Marie Read; 65 (above) Bruce Coleman Collection © Pacific Stock (below), Ardea London (left) © Bill Coster, (below right) © Ron and Valerie Taylor; 68 Mary Evans Picture Library; 80 (above) Bruce Coleman Collection © Dr.Hermann Brehm, (below) American Museum of Natural History, New York, (Special Collections); 86 (left) University of Michigan Exhibit Museum, (right) & 87 Vincent L Morgan and Katherine P Morgan, The Granger Papers Project; 88 (above) Bruce Coleman Collection © Alain Compost, (below) Oxford Scientific Films © Stan Osolinski; 96 University of Michigan Exhibit Museum © (above) Holly Smith; 104 (above) © BBC 2001; 105 (left) Bruce Coleman Collection © Joe McDonald, (right) Ardea London © Liz Bomford; 107 Fortean Picture Library, (centre) © Richard Svensson, (below) © Tony Healy; 116 Scott E Foss, John Day Fossil Beds National Monument, Oregon; 121 (left) The Art of Wildlife Images © Frank Krahmer, (right) © Peter Dazeley; 130–1 Courtesy of the Department of Library Services, American Museum of Natural History, New York, (Special Collections) photos: Shackelford; 133 (above) Robert Harding Picture Library, (below) © Dick Mol;140 Robert Harding Picture Library (left) ©Jeremy Lightfoot, (right) © Robert Francis;146 (above) Bruce Coleman Collection © Anders Blomqvist; 147 (above) Ardea London © François Gohier, (below) Sylvia Cordaiy Photo Library; 150 (above) With the Kind Permission of The Royal Photographic Society Picture Library, Bath photo: Muybridge, (below) Oxford Scientific Films © Konrad Wothe; 153 (above centre) Science Photo Library © Sheila Terry (above right) Still Pictures © Roland Seitre (below) Oxford Scientific Films © Steve Turner; 154 Science Photo Library (above) © Rocher Jerrican, (below) © John Reader, (below right) © Volker Steger/Nordstar; 168 (above) Ardea London © François Gohier, (below left) Department of Palaeontology and Palaeo-environmental Studies, Transvaal Museum, Pretoria, South Africa, (below right) Natural History Museum, London; 172 Ardea London (above) © M. Neugebauer, (below) © Kenneth W Fink; 176 (above left) Institute of Human Origins, Arizona State University © Enrico Ferorelli; 176–7 Science Photo Library © John Reader; 186 (above) Ardea London © Yves Bilat;186–7 Robert Harding Picture Library © Frans Lanting, (right) Ardea London © K.W. Fink; 190 (above) BBC Natural History Unit Picture Library © C. Seddon, (below) Courtesy of the George C. Page Museum, Los Angeles © Ed Ikuta; 201 (left) Ardea London © Adrian Warren, (right) Bruce Coleman Collection © Stattan Widstrand; 212 Natural History Museum, London; 213 (left) The University of Leeds, School of Biology (right) Still Pictures © Jany Sauvenet; 216 Mary Evans Picture Library; 224 (above) Still Pictures © François Pierrel; 225 Ardea London (left) © M Watson, (right) © François Gohier, 236 (above) Hulton Archive (below) Novosti Photo Library; 237 Ardea London (above) © Masahiro Iijima; 239 © Instituto Português de Arqueologia, Lisbon; 249 (left) Dr. Hartmut Thieme, Niedersächsisches Landesverwaltungsamt, Institut für Denkmalpflege, Hanover, Germany, (right) Werner Forman Archive/Tanzania National Museum, Dar es Salaam; 253 (below left) Science Photo Library © D.A. Peel, (above right) Bruce Coleman Collection © Astrofoto, (below right) Ardea London © Jean-Paul Ferrero; 254 (above) Science Photo Library/Nairobi National Museum © Sinclair Stammers, (below) Werner Forman Archive/British Museum, (below right) Natural History Museum.